THE
One & Only
asian
Cookbook

THE One & Only asian Cookbook

All the recipes you will ever need

With a foreword by
Jenny Linford

WELDONOWEN
PUBLISHING

WELDONOWEN
PUBLISHING

First published in the UK by
Weldon Owen Ltd., an imprint of the Bonnier Group
The Plaza
535 King's Road
London
SW10 0SZ
www.weldonowen.co.uk
www.bonnierpublishing.com

ISBN-13: 978 1 78342 218 0

A catalogue record for this book is available from the
British Library

Printed and bound by Interak, Poland
10 9 8 7 6 5 4 3 2 1

"Do not dismiss the dish by saying that it is just simple food. The blessed thing is an entire civilisation in itself!"

Abdulhak Sinasi

Contents

Foreword

By Jenny Linford

The world of Asian cuisine is an exciting and vibrant one, packed with vivid flavours, textures and colours. Asian dishes range from tempting deep-fried nibbles or textured salads to speedily made noodle dishes or slow-simmered, fragrant curries. Characteristic tastes range from the mildness of coconut milk or delicate bean curd (tofu) to the aromatic heat of root ginger or the explosive piquancy of red chillies. Once you've got the taste for this truly diverse cuisine and discovered how simple it is to cook at home, you'll thoroughly enjoy exploring it.

Key Techniques

One of the striking things about Asian cuisine is the range of cooking techniques it encompasses: shallow-frying, stir-frying, deep-frying, steaming and braising, to name but a few. Once you've grasped the principles of these core techniques, then you can use them to create a huge range of dishes.

Making curry pastes

While ready-made curry pastes are a speedy option, making your own curry paste is simple and offers far more scope. Core ingredients are onion, garlic and root ginger, with ingredients such as lemon grass, fresh chillies and galangal (an aromatic rhizome like ginger) also used in Thai and Malaysian pastes. Traditionally these would have been pounded together in a pestle and mortar. Nowadays, using a food processor instead saves a lot of labour! This basic paste can then be flavoured with different combinations of ground spices depending on the recipe.

Cook your curry paste well

Many curry recipes required you to fry the paste. Make sure that you cook your paste thoroughly and for long enough – a good 5–10 minutes – to remove any 'rawness' from it before you add in the other ingredients. To prevent it burning use a heavy-based pan, add in enough oil, and stir it constantly as it cooks.

Dry-fry your spices

One simple way to increase the flavour of your spiced dishes is by dry-frying or 'roasting' your whole spices beforehand. Simply heat a heavy-based frying pan, **without** adding any oil or fat in, add in the spices and fry over a medium heat for

1–2 minutes, stirring often, until they smell fragrant. Keep an eye on them as spices burn quickly. Remove, cool and either use whole or grind as required.

Cooking with coconut

In much of Asian food, coconut milk (made by crushing coconut flesh in water) stands in for dairy, used to add a creamy texture and mellow flavour to dishes such as curries. Fresh coconut milk is hard to find outside Asia, but, when it comes to cooking, frozen coconut milk or tinned coconut milk are excellent substitutes. Coconut milk made from creamed coconut block diluted with water is less successful when it comes to cooking. Thick coconut milk can easily curdle, so stir it as you bring it to the boil to prevent this.

The secret to successful stir-frying

This famous Chinese cooking technique from Canton consists of frying chopped ingredients in a wok over a high heat, resulting in fresh-tasting, textured food in a matter of minutes. For good results:

Chop your ingredients into small, even-sized pieces to ensure that they cook through in the short cooking time.

Make sure that all your chopping and preparation is complete **before** you start cooking.

Cooking over a high heat is essential for successful stir-frying. Make sure that you heat your wok thoroughly over a high heat before you start stir-frying.

Use a spatula to keep the ingredients moving.

Stock up your store cupboard

If you enjoy cooking Asian dishes, then it's well worth stocking up on the key ingredients, so that you have them readily to hand. Usually a good source of high-quality, reasonably priced authentic ingredients are the food shops that serve that community, so look out for Chinese, Indian, Japanese or Thai food stores and investigate what they have.

A core range of spices for curries includes: ground turmeric, cumin (whole and ground), coriander (whole and ground), chili powder, dried whole chillies, cinnamon sticks and cardamom pods. Store the spices in airtight containers in a cool, dark place and they will keep well for months.

Other Asian ingredients to have in your cupboards and freezer: tinned coconut milk, soy sauce, Thai fish sauce, oyster sauce, Chinese rice wine or Amontillado sherry, chili sauce, tamarind pulp or paste, blachan (Malay shrimp paste), wasabi paste, miso paste, assorted noodles, basmati rice, root ginger, garlic, frozen kaffir lime leaves and frozen curry leaves.

Banana spring rolls with toffee sauce

1. Mix the bananas with the lime juice and zest, cinnamon, vanilla syrup and brown sugar. Set aside.

2. Make a sugar syrup by combining the sugar and water and gently bringing to the boil until the sugar has dissolved. Lower the heat and simmer for a few minutes before removing from the heat.

3. Heat the oven to 400°F (200°C).

4. Assemble the spring rolls by placing a heaped teaspoon of the banana mixture slightly off centre on a spring roll wrapper. Brush around the edges of the wrapper with the sugar syrup. Fold the bottom corner of the spring roll over the filling and then fold in the opposite 2 corners and roll the spring roll as tightly as possible.

5. Place the spring rolls on a baking tray and brush each with a little of the melted butter. Cook in the oven for around 20 –25 minutes or until golden brown.

6. Serve immediately with toffee sauce for dipping.

Preparation time: 15 min
Cooking time: 25 min
Serves 12–14

4 bananas, roughly chopped
juice and zest of 1 lime
1 tsp cinnamon
2 tsp vanilla syrup
2 tbsp light brown sugar
75g white sugar
100ml water
12–14 medium–sized spring roll
  wrappers
50g melted butter
ready–made toffee sauce

Lamb biryani

1. Mix together the marinade ingredients. Add the lamb and mix well. Set aside for at least 2 hours.

2. Soak the rice in 1½ litres of water for 3 hours. Heat the milk with the saffron and cardamom until hot. Turn off the heat and leave to infuse whilst you prepare the rest of the dish.

3. Heat the oven to 400°F (200°C).

4. Add a little oil to a frying pan and add the onion, cashew nuts and garam masala. Cook until the onion is tinged golden. Drain the rice and add to the pan along with the sultanas. Continue cooking for 1½ minutes.

5. Drizzle the bottom of a large flameproof baking dish with oil. Top with a layer of rice, a layer of the lamb yoghurt mixture and a little of the milk. Continue layering until the rice, lamb and milk are all used.

6. Wrap lightly in a foil and bake for 40–50 minutes.

Preparation time: 20 min
   plus 3 h marinating and
   soaking
Cooking time: 50 min
Serves 4

400g lamb leg steak, trimmed of fat
   and diced
250g basmati rice
200ml milk
1 tsp saffron
4 cardamoms
groundnut oil
1 medium onion, finely sliced
30g cashew nuts
1 tsp garam masala
2 tbsp golden sultanas

For the marinade:
100g plain yoghurt
3 garlic cloves
1 tsp chilli powder
1 tsp ground coriander
1 tsp ground cumin
1 tsp cinnamon
40g minced ginger

Green papaya salad and chicken with sesame lime dressing

1. Heat a little oil in a frying pan. Add the chicken and cook until tender, making sure you break it up as it cooks. When the mince is cooked, add half the mint and coriander.

2. Mix together the papaya, carrot, spring onion, sesame seeds and the rest of the basil and mint.

3. Mix together the dressing ingredients. Add half to the papaya mixture and the remaining half to the chicken.

4. Take a large serving platter and top with the papaya. Add the chicken over it.

Preparation time: 30 min
Cooking time: 10 min
Serves 4 as a starter

Sesame oil
200g minced chicken
bunch of mint, shredded
bunch of coriander, roughly chopped
240g green papaya, chopped into
  matchsticks
1 large carrot, chopped into
  matchsticks
1 spring onion, chopped into
  matchsticks
1 tbsp toasted sesame seeds

For the dressing:
2 red chillies, finely chopped
2 tbsp minced ginger
3 tbsp soya sauce
3 tbsp fish sauce
2 shallots, finely sliced
juice of 2 limes
6 tbsp sesame oil
1 tsp sugar

Mango, lime and passion fruit ice lollies

Preparation time: 4 h
Serves 4 to 6 lollies
 depending on size of moulds

2 ripe mangoes
juice of 2 limes and zest of 1
175g sugar
170ml water
3 passion fruits

1. Peel the mangoes and remove the seeds. Add the mango to a food processor and blend until smooth. Add in the lime juice and zest.

2. Make a sugar syrup by combining the sugar and water in a small pan. Heat the sugar and water and stir until dissolved, this should take around 2–3 minutes.

3. Add some of the sugar syrup to the mango a little at a time, testing the mixture until you have reached your desired sweetness.

4. Remove the pulp from the passion fruits and combine with 3 tablespoons of the mango mixture.

5. Add the passion fruit mixture to your lolly moulds and place in the freezer for about 1 hour or until frozen. Top up the lolly moulds with the mango mixture and place back in the freezer for a further 2 hours or until frozen.

Nasi Goreng

1. Using a non–stick frying pan, heat some oil and pour in the egg to make a very thin omelette. Once cooked, slide it out of the pan. Roll and slice into ribbons.

2. Add more oil to the pan and fry the chicken and chilli paste. Cook for 5 minutes before adding the shallots, carrot, garlic, peanuts and water chestnuts. Continue cooking for a further 4 minutes. Add the rice, soy sauce, fish sauce and lime juice. Stir in the chopped coriander.

3. Spoon into bowls to serve topping with the egg ribbons and some cucumber strips.

Preparation time: 5 min
Cooking time: 20 min
Serves 4

sesame oil
3 eggs, whisked
400g chicken breast, cut into cubes
4 tbsp chilli paste
4 shallots, finely sliced
1 carrot, shredded
4 garlic cloves, crushed
80g natural peanuts, unroasted or
    salted, roughly chopped
80g water chestnuts
240g dry rice (60g per person),
    cooked and chilled.
8 tbsp soy sauce
8 tbsp fish sauce
juice of 1 lime
small bunch of coriander, roughly
    chopped
¼ cucumber, cut into strips

Bream with ginger sauce

1. Season the fish with salt and pepper. Put into a pan with the lemon, spring onion, half the ginger and water. Bring to a boil and simmer until the fish is cooked. The fish is cooked when the eyes bulge out. Remove the fish and keep it warm in a low oven.

2. For the sauce: heat the oil in a pan, add the remaining ginger and cook gently for 1 minute.

3. Add the wine, stock, soy sauce, sugar, vinegar and salt and bring to a boil.

4. Dissolve the lotus root starch in 4–5 tablespoons cold water and stir into the boiling sauce. Pour half the sauce into a small serving dish. Strain the rest of the sauce through a sieve.

5. Place the fish on a serving plate and place the drained ginger on top of the fish. Pour the sieved sauce around the fish.

6. Garnish with bundles of shredded leek in chilli rings, chilli 'flowers' and coriander.

Preparation time: 10 min
Cooking time: 20 min
Serves 4

2 bream, (approx. 600g), cleaned and scaled
salt and pepper to taste
½ lemon
1 spring onion, sliced
100g ginger, finely chopped

For the ginger sauce:
3 tbsp oil
1 tbsp rice wine
300ml vegetable stock
2 tbsp soy sauce
3 tbsp sugar
4 tbsp brown rice vinegar
2 tsp salt
2 tbsp lotus root starch

To garnish:
½ leek (white part only) finely shredded
2–4 chillies, sliced into rings
4 chillies, slit open to make 'flowers'
coriander leaves

Diced salmon with soy dip

1. For the marinade: mix together all the ingredients and marinate the salmon cubes for about 30 minutes.

2. Heat the grill.

3. Remove the salmon from the marinade and grill for 2–3 minutes until lightly browned. Brush with the marinade from time to time.

4. For the dip: mix together all the ingredients and season to taste with salt and pepper.

5. Pour the dip over the salmon.

Preparation time: 15 min
   plus 30 min marinating
Cooking time: 5 min
Serves 4

*500g skinless salmon fillets, cut
   into bite-sized cubes*

*For the marinade:
juice and zest of 2 lemons
1 tbsp wholegrain mustard
1 tbsp olive oil*

*For the dip:
5 tbsp light soy sauce
1 red chilli, finely chopped
1 spring onion, sliced
1 tbsp chopped coriander leaves*

Chinese vegetable stir-fry with cuttlefish

Preparation time: 10 min
Cooking time: 15 min
Serves 4

400g cuttlefish tubes, cut into
  strips
2 tbsp sesame oil
3 garlic cloves, finely chopped
2 tsp grated ginger
200g mangetout
400g green peppers, cut into
  thin strips
4 tbsp soy sauce
150g oyster sauce
4 tbsp rice wine
125ml chicken stock
1 ½ tbsp cornflour

1. Blanch the cuttlefish strips in boiling water for 3 minutes. Drain well and set aside.

2. Heat the sesame oil in a wok or a large frying pan. Cook the garlic, ginger, mangetout and peppers for 1–2 minutes until softened.

3. Pour in the soy sauce, oyster sauce, rice wine and chicken stock, bring to a boil and simmer for 1 minute.

4. Mix the cornflour to a smooth paste with a little cold water, stir in and bring to a boil. Cook, stirring, until thickened.

5. Add the cuttlefish strips. Mix well and bring back to a boil. Season to taste with salt and pepper.

Peking duck with plum sauce

1. Place the duck on a rack in a deep roasting tin. Pour over the boiling water and set aside until the water has drained away from the bird. Discard the water and leave the duck exposed to air until dry.

2. Mix together the honey, soy sauce, five spice powder and brown sugar. Brush the sauce over the duck, inside and out. Leave the bird to dry. Brush the sauce over the duck again and leave to dry. Repeat the process until all the sauce has been used.

3. Heat the oven to 200°C (400°F).

4. Cook the duck for 30 minutes, then turn it over and cook for a further 30 minutes, until the skin is crisp. Remove from the oven and leave to cool for 15 minutes. Joint the duck and slice off the meat.

5. For the sauce: mix together the sesame oil, hoisin sauce, sugar, water, soy sauce and cornflour. Heat in a wok or frying pan until simmering. Cook, stirring, until the sauce has thickened. Leave to cool.

6. For the pancakes: warm the pancakes in a bamboo steamer for 4 minutes. Spread 1 teaspoon sauce over each pancake and scatter some spring onions and cucumber. Divide the sliced duck meat between the pancakes. Roll up the pancakes and pour the remaining sauce over them.

Preparation time: 20 min
  plus drying time
Cooking time: 1 h 15 min
Serves 8 pancakes

1 whole duck
2 litres boiling water
5 tbsp clear honey
2 tbsp dark soy sauce
4 tbsp Chinese five spice powder
2 tbsp light brown sugar

For the sauce:
2 tbsp sesame oil
6 tbsp hoisin sauce
6 tbsp sugar
6 tbsp water
1 tbsp dark soy sauce
1 tbsp cornflour

For the pancakes:
8 pancakes, ready–made
4 spring onions, shredded
1 small cucumber, cut into sticks

Asian cashew nut and chicken stir-fry

1. Cook the rice according to the directions on the pack.

2. Mix together the egg, soy sauce and cornflour into a smooth paste. Season with pepper, add the chicken and stir well.

3. Heat 1 teaspoon oil in a wok or frying pan and fry the cashew nuts until just browned. Pat dry with kitchen paper.

4. Heat the remaining oil in the wok. Add the chicken and fry in batches on a high flame until golden. Remove and set aside.

5. Add the cashew nuts and garlic to the pan and cook for 1 minute. Add the chicken and cook gently for 5 minutes.

6. Drain the rice and put into serving bowls. Divide the chicken mixture between serving bowls and garnish with spring onions.

Preparation time: 10 min
Cooking time: 15 min
Serves 4

250g basmati rice
1 egg
3 tbsp soy sauce
1 tbsp cornflour
600g chicken breast, finely chopped
2 tbsp peanut oil
200g lightly salted cashew nuts
1 garlic clove, finely crushed

To garnish:
1 spring onion, cut into thin strips

Fried Sichuan-style tofu cubes

1. Cut the tofu into 4cm cubes.

2. Heat the oil in a wok or frying pan, add the soy sauce and salt and cook for 1 minute, then add the chilli powder and cook for another 30 seconds.

3. Stir in the stock, add the tofu and simmer for 3 minutes.

4. Mix the cornflour with 1 tablespoon water and add the garlic. Cook for 1 minute.

5. Pour some sauce over the tofu and sprinkle with Sichuan pepper.

Preparation time: 10 min
Cooking time: 6 min
Serves 4

500g tofu
1 tbsp peanut oil
2 tbsp soy sauce
pinch salt
½ tsp chilli powder
200ml chicken stock
2 tsp cornflour
2 tbsp finely chopped garlic cloves
1 tsp ground Sichuan pepper

Bhuna Gosht – lamb in a spicy tomato-curry sauce

1. Mix the ginger with the garam masala and rub the mixture into the lamb chunks. Marinate at room temperature for at least 30 minutes.

2. Heat 2 tablespoons oil in a large pan and fry the onions, garlic and chilli pepper on a gentle flame until softened but not brown. Stir in the cumin and paprika and season with salt and pepper, cook for 2 minutes then remove the mixture from the pan and set aside.

3. Heat the remaining oil in the pan and fry the lamb on a medium flame on all sides for 5 minutes.

4. Pour the tomato paste into the pan, add the onion mixture and pour over 750ml water.

5. Bring to a boil, then reduce the flame and cook very gently, stirring occasionally, for 1 hour or until the meat is tender.

6. Check the seasoning and divide the meat between 4 bowls. Garnish with the coriander, tomatoes and yoghurt.

Preparation time: 15 min
  plus 30 min marinating
Cooking time: 1 h 15 min
Serves 4

*thumb–size piece fresh ginger,
  peeled and chopped*
1 tbsp garam masala
800g lean lamb, cut into large chunks
6 tbsp vegetable oil
4 onions, diced
2 garlic cloves, sliced
*1 green chilli pepper, deseeded and
  finely chopped*
½ tsp ground cumin
1 tsp paprika
2 tbsp tomato paste
*8 sprigs coriander leaves and stalks,
  finely chopped*
3 tomatoes, diced
4 tbsp plain yoghurt

Tandoori fish masala

1. Heat the oven to 190°C (375°F). Grease a shallow baking dish with the ghee.

2. Rub the fish with salt and lemon juice and place in the dish.

3. For the marinade: mix all the ingredients with 1–2 tablespoons water and pour over the fish. Cover and marinate in the refrigerator for about 2 hours, turning occasionally.

4. Cook for 15–20 minutes, until the fish is cooked. If necessary, add some more water during cooking so the dish doesn't dry out.

5. Heat the grill.

6. Place the dish under the grill for a few minutes, until the fish has browned slightly.

7. Place in individual bowls with the chilli, shallot and lime zest sprinkled on top.

Preparation time: 10 min
  plus 2 h marinating
Cooking time: 25 min
Serves 4

2 tbsp melted ghee
600g fish fillets, eg. cod; cut into
  large pieces
2 tbsp lemon juice

For the marinade:
400ml plain yoghurt
3 tbsp vinegar
1 large onion, finely grated
4 garlic cloves, crushed
1 walnut-size piece ginger, grated
1 tsp turmeric
1 pinch salt
1 pinch ground coriander
1 pinch garam masala
1 pinch chilli powder

To garnish:
½ red chilli, cut into rings
1 tbsp shallot, cut into rings
1 tbsp grated lime zest

Oranges in syrup

Preparation time: 10 min
   plus overnight standing
Cooking time: 10 min
Serves 4

4 oranges
100g brown sugar
250ml water
2cm piece ginger, sliced
4cl orange liqueur
mint leaves, to serve

1. Peel the oranges, removing all the white pith and cut into slices about 0.5–1cm thick.

2. Mix the sugar in a pan with the water, bring to a boil and simmer for 10 minutes. Remove from the flame and leave to cool.

3. Add the ginger and orange liqueur and put the orange slices into the syrup. Cover and leave to stand overnight.

4. Remove the orange slices from the syrup and decorate with mint.

Dan dan Sichuan noodles

1. For the meat topping: heat the peanut oil in a wok or frying pan over a medium flame.

2. When the oil is hot, add the chillies and Sichuan pepper and stir–fry for 30 seconds.

3. Add the ya cai or preserved vegetable and continue to stir–fry for 2 minutes.

4. Add the beef and fry for 10 minutes until the meat is browned all over.

5. Splash in the soy sauce and stir–fry for a further 10 minutes, until the meat is brown and a little crisp. Season with salt to taste.

6. Bring a pan of salted water to a boil. Add the noodles and cook for 4 minutes until tender.

7. For the sauce: mix together the Sichuan pepper, light and dark soy sauce and chilli oil. **8.** Drain the noodles. Divide the meat between 4 bowls, top with the noodles and drizzle over the sauce.

9. Garnish with the chopped spring onion.

Preparation time: 10 min
Cooking time: 25 min
Serves 4

For the meat topping:
1 tbsp peanut oil
3 dried chillies, halved and seeds
discarded
½ tsp whole Sichuan pepper
25g Sichuan ya cai or preserved
mustard leaves
100g minced beef
2 tsp light soy sauce
300g dried wide Chinese noodles

For the sauce:
1 tsp ground roasted Sichuan pepper
1 tbsp light soy sauce
1 tbsp dark soy sauce
2 tbsp chilli oil

To garnish:
1 spring onion, finely chopped

Fish cakes with coriander and tamarind

1. For the chilli sauce: crush the peppers, garlic and chilli in a mortar. Put into a small pan with the water, vinegar, lime juice and sugar and bring to a boil. Simmer gently for 15 minutes.

2. For the fishcakes: heat the coconut milk and soak the bread in the milk.

3. Heat the oil in a frying pan and cook the spring onions and tamarind pulp for 2–3 minutes until softened.

4. Squeeze out the bread and mix with the fish. Stir in the spring onions, ginger, egg yolks and coriander. Season to taste with salt and pepper. Form into 8 cakes using wet hands.

5. Heat the oil in a frying pan and fry the fishcakes for about 5 minutes on each side, until golden brown.

6. Serve the chilli sauce with the fish cakes. Garnish with lime wedges and coriander leaves.

Preparation time: 15 min
Cooking time: 25 min

For the chilli sauce:
½ red pepper, diced
1 garlic clove, finely chopped
2 red chilli peppers, finely chopped
200ml water
50ml red wine vinegar
2 tbsp lime juice
1 tbsp sugar
For the fishcakes:
150ml coconut milk
100g sliced white bread
1 tbsp oil
4 spring onions, sliced
2 tsp tamarind pulp, finely chopped
600g cod fillet, chopped
2 tsp grated ginger
2 egg yolks
1 tbsp chopped coriander leaves
200ml vegetable oil
To garnish:
lime wedges
coriander leaves

Prawn cakes with spicy sauce

1. Peel the prawns and remove the heads. Remove the intestinal vein and chop the prawn meat very finely.

2. Crush the garlic, chili and coriander in a mortar with salt and pepper. Add the prawn meat and work to a paste.

3. Add the egg and mix well. Form the mixture into approximately 5cm patties, using 2 tablespoons of the mixture for each one.

4. Heat the oil in a deep pan and fry the prawn cakes for about 2 minutes, until golden brown. Drain on kitchen paper. Serve with the spicy sweet and sour sauce.

Preparation time: 15 min
Cooking time: 5 min
Serves 4

800g prawns
3 garlic cloves
1 chilli, seeds removed
2 sprigs coriander
½ tsp salt and pepper
1 egg, whisked
500ml vegetable oil
1 jar spicy sweet and sour sauce

Gado gado with peanut dressing

Preparation time: 25 min
Serves 4

2 shallots, finely chopped
1 garlic clove, finely chopped
60g peanut butter
100ml coconut milk
2 tsp cane sugar
4 tbsp soy sauce
2 tbsp lemon juice
1 tsp sambal oelek
300ml plain yoghurt
200g iceberg lettuce, torn
100g white cabbage, shredded
1 cucumber, peeled and thinly
   sliced
4 small tomatoes, thinly sliced
150g mung bean sprouts
2 hard-boiled eggs, quartered

1. Mix the shallots and garlic with the peanut butter and coconut milk and season to taste with sugar, soy sauce, lemon juice and sambal oelek. Stir in the yoghurt.

2. Line serving plates with the lettuce leaves and shredded cabbage. Arrange the cucumber, tomatoes and bean sprouts on top of the lettuce.

3. Spoon the peanut sauce on top and garnish with the quartered eggs.

Chicken jalfrezi

1. Chop the meat into thin strips and mix with the Worcestershire sauce.

2. Heat the oil in a frying pan and fry the mustard seeds and cumin seeds, stirring, for about 30 seconds, until they start to pop.

3. Add the onions and chillies and fry, stirring, until the onions are lightly browned.

4. Stir in the chicken, Worcestershire sauce, ground spices, sugarsnap peas and peas and season to taste with salt and pepper.

5. Add the water, bring to a boil and cook over a medium flame for a further 3–5 minutes, stirring, until the meat and vegetables are just cooked. Add coconut cream to taste.

6. Divide into 4 bowls and sprinkle with mint.

Preparation time: 10 min
Cooking time: 15 min
Serves 4

500g chicken breast fillets, cut into
  strips
1 tbsp Worcestershire sauce
3 tbsp oil
1 pinch brown mustard seeds
1 pinch cumin seeds
3 onions, sliced
2 red chillies, finely chopped
1 pinch ground cumin
1 pinch coriander
1 pinch turmeric
200g sugarsnap peas
150g peas
220ml water
150–200ml coconut cream
mint leaves

Rice paper cones filled with chicken and Asian vegetables

1. Soak the rice paper between the damp tea towels.

2. Blanch the mangetout in salted boiling water for 3 minutes. Drain and rinse in cold water.

3. Season the chicken breast fillets with salt and pepper. Heat the butter and fry the chicken breasts over a medium flame for about 5 minutes on each side. Remove and slice thinly at an angle.

4. Mix together the vinegar and oil and season to taste with salt and pepper.

5. Fold the sheets of rice paper in half to form a triangle. Divide the vegetables, mushrooms, chicken and basil leaves between each triangle. Sprinkle with the dressing and carefully fold the ends round to make a cone.

Preparation time: 15 min
Cooking time: 10 min
Serves 4

4 sheets rice paper
100g mangetout
2 chicken breast fillets
1 tbsp butter
1 tbsp white wine vinegar
3 tbsp olive oil
½ bunch spring onions, cut into thin strips
1 carrot, cut into thin strips
50g enokitake mushrooms
basil leaves

Deseeding a chilli

Chillies come in a wide range of flavours and heats, but the heat is in the seeds and ribs, so for a milder flavour, you need to remove them. The alkaloid in chillies can cause irritation, so always wear gloves or wash your hands well after deseeding chillies.

STEP 1 Chop off and remove the stalk end of the chilli using a sharp knife, then cut the chilli in half lengthways.

STEP 2 Press open each half of the chilli and, using a teaspoon, scrape away the seeds and the white ribs and discard.

STEP 3 Holding down the broader, stalk end of each chilli half, cut the flesh into long vertical strips.

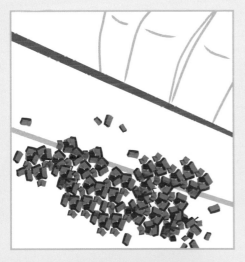

STEP 4 Cut across the strips to make small cubes, holding down the chilli with the other hand, moving it as you go.

STEP 5 Chillies also make pretty 'flower' garnishes; cut vertical strips from the stalk downwards, leaving the stalk on.

Rogan Josh

1. Mix the ginger and garlic together to form a coarse powder.

2. Heat the oil in a large frying pan and cook the cardamom, cinnamon and bay leaves. Add the meat and fry until browned, then remove from the pan.

3. Add the onions and the ginger-garlic mixture to the pan and fry gently until the onions are translucent. Stir in the cumin, coriander, cayenne pepper, paprika and tomato purée and cook for a further 2 minutes.

4. Place the meat back in the pan, add the water, bring to a boil and simmer for 1 hour.

Preparation time: 15 min
Cooking time: 1 h 10 min
Serves 4

1 walnut-size piece ginger, grated
6 garlic cloves, crushed
6 tbsp peanut oil
8 cardamom pods
3cm stick cinnamon
2 bay leaves
800g lamb, cut into bite-sized pieces
2 onions, chopped
2 tsp cumin seeds, crushed
2 tsp ground coriander
pinch cayenne pepper, more if
  desired
1 tbsp sweet paprika
1–2 tbsp tomato purée
300ml water

Spring rolls

1. Mix together the shallot, chilli, garlic, carrot and bean sprouts.

2. Drain the mushrooms and chop them finely. Drain the noodles and rinse in cold water. Drain and chop.

3. Mix the mushrooms, noodles and pork with the shallot mixture and stir in the shrimps.

4. Lay the spring roll sheets out and divide the filling between the sheets, placing it in the centre.

5. Brush the edges with egg white and roll up.

6. Heat the oil in a deep pan and fry the spring rolls in batches for 2–3 minutes until golden brown and crisp. Drain on kitchen paper.

7. Garnish with herbs and Nuoc Cham sauce.

Preparation time: 25 min
Cooking time: 5 min
Serves 4

1 shallot, finely chopped
1 red chilli, finely chopped
1 garlic clove, finely chopped
1 carrot, grated
50g bean sprouts
2 dried shiitake mushrooms, soaked
   in warm water for 30 minutes
50g rice noodles, soaked in hot water
   for 5 minutes
200g minced pork
125g raw, peeled shrimp tails,
   chopped
8 spring roll sheets, (20 x 20cm)
1 egg white, whisked
oil, for deep frying

To garnish:
2 sprigs coriander
2 sprigs mint
120ml Nuoc Cham sauce

Miso soup with wakame seaweed and silken tofu

1. Put the dashi and bonito flakes into a pan with the water and bring to a boil. Leave to infuse for 10 minutes, then strain, retaining the liquid.

2. Stir the miso pastes into the liquid and bring to a boil.

3. Add the mushrooms, tofu and wakame and return to a boil.

4. Ladle into bowls and garnish with spring onion.

Preparation time: 10 min
  plus 10 min infusing
Cooking time: 15 min
Serves 4

2 pieces dashi seaweed
4 tbsp bonito flakes
1 litre water
4 tsp light miso paste
2 tsp miso paste
100g shiitake mushrooms, sliced
40g silken tofu, diced
2 tsp wakame,
fine strips of spring onion

Seafood curry with shrimp and mango

Preparation time: 10 min
Cooking time: 20 min
Serves 4

2 mangoes, peeled and sliced
3 tbsp grated coconut
3 tbsp coconut milk
good pinch chilli powder
2 tbsp curry powder
2 tbsp oil
3 tbsp water
1 carrot, diced
2 onions, diced
3 garlic cloves, finely chopped
2 stalks celery, diced
500g large shrimps
sesame oil
juice of ½ lemon
celery leaves, to serve

1. Put half the mango slices into a blender with the grated coconut, coconut milk, chilli powder, curry powder and water and blend to a fine purée.

2. Heat the oil in a pan and cook the diced vegetables for 4 minutes. Add the shrimps and cook for 2–3 minutes.

3. Stir in the puréed mango sauce and simmer gently for 8 minutes. If the sauce becomes too thick, thin with a little coconut milk or warm water.

4. Season the curry with sesame oil, lemon juice, salt and pepper to taste.

5. Serve garnished with the remaining mango slices and celery leaves.

Chickpea korma

1. For the spice mixture: mix together the onions, garlic, chilli, ginger and almonds.

2. Melt the ghee in a wok or frying pan and add the cardamom, cinnamon, cumin and coriander and gently fry together. Stirring continuously, add the onion-spice mixture and cook for 2–3 minutes.

3. Add the coconut milk and chickpeas and simmer uncovered for 20 minutes, stirring occasionally.

4. Cook the rice according to the directions on the pack.

5. Stir the garam masala into the pan and season to taste with salt.

6. Drain the rice and place on serving plates. Spoon the korma on top. Garnish with spring onion rings.

Preparation time: 10 min
Cooking time: 25 min
Serves 4

For the spice mixture:
2 onions, finely chopped
3 garlic cloves, finely chopped
2 red chilli peppers, cut into rings
1 tsp fresh root ginger, grated
50g ground almonds

Plus:
2 tbsp ghee
pinch ground cardamom
½ tsp ground cinnamon
1 ½ tsp ground cumin
1 tsp ground coriander
400ml coconut milk
250g tinned chickpeas
250g basmati rice
1 ½ tsp garam masala

To garnish:
1 spring onion, sliced into rings.

Red chicken curry with chillies and rice

1. Toss the chicken in the cornflour to coat.

2. For the red curry paste: put all the ingredients in a food processor and process to a paste.

3. Heat the oil in a wok or frying pan and quickly brown the meat. Add the onion, garlic, lime leaves and chillies. Stir in the coconut milk, curry paste, sugar and fish sauce. Cover and cook over a low flame for 20–25 minutes until the chicken is cooked through.

4. Stir the coriander leaves into the curry before serving.

5. Garnish with chillies, basil and coriander leaves.

Cooking time: 45 min
Serves 4

800g breast fillets, cubed
2 tsp cornflour
2 tbsp oil
1 onion, finely chopped
2 garlic cloves, finely chopped
2 lime leaves, shredded
2 red chillies, finely chopped
250ml unsweetened coconut milk
2 tbsp red curry paste
1 tsp sugar
1 tbsp fish sauce
1 tbsp shredded coriander leaves

To garnish:
red chillies
basil leaves
coriander leaves

For the red curry paste:
5 dried, red chillies, deseeded and soaked
5 shallots, finely chopped
10 garlic cloves, chopped
1 tsp finely chopped galangal
1 tbsp chopped lemon grass
1 tsp finely chopped kaffir lime leaves
2 tsp finely chopped coriander root
5 peppercorns
1 tbsp coriander seeds, toasted
1 tsp cumin seeds, toasted
1 tsp salt
1 tsp prawn paste

Sweet maki with marzipan and melon

1. Heat the olive oil in a wide shallow pan, add the rice and toss to coat in the oil. Add the milk and cook slowly, stirring until the milk is absorbed and the rice is soft. Stir in the chocolate and leave to cool.

2. Knead the marzipan with the icing sugar and food colouring. Roll out on a surface dusted with icing sugar to 25 x 9cm. Place on a sheet of non-stick baking paper.

3. Spread the risotto evenly on the rolled-out marzipan and press on firmly, leaving about 1cm free on the narrow side.

4. Lay the melon down the middle of the rice and roll up the marzipan and rice from the long side to form a sushi roll, using the paper to help you. Chill for 2 hours.

5. Remove the paper from the roll and cut into 2cm lengths.

6. Mix the candied orange peel with the orange juice and put into a small bowl. Serve with the sweet sushi rolls.

Preparation time: 15 min
  plus 2 h chilling
Cooking time: 35 min
Serves 4

1 tbsp olive oil
100g risotto rice
200ml milk
70g white chocolate, chopped
50g marzipan
50g icing sugar
green food colouring
½ sweet melon, cut into 7mm
  squares
juice of 1 orange
candied orange peel, cut into
  thin strips

Chinese chicken salad in won ton shells

Preparation time: 20 min
  plus 2 h marinating
Cooking time: 20 min
Serves 10–12 won tons

2 garlic cloves, finely chopped
1 tbsp diced onion
1 pinch ground lemon grass
1 pinch mixture of anise,
  coriander and cumin
2 tbsp light soy sauce
4 tbsp coconut milk
4 chicken breast fillets
250g ready-made won ton pastry
oil, for deep frying

To garnish:
spring onion leaves
coriander leaves

1. Mix together the garlic, onion, lemon grass, spices, soy sauce, coconut milk and a sprinkling of salt and pepper. Marinate the chicken in the mixture for 2 hours.

2. Divide the pastry into 10–12 squares. Heat the oil to about 180°C (350°F).

3. Press the pastry squares into a small metal sieve to form small pastry shells and deep-fry in oil in batches until golden brown. Drain on kitchen paper.

4. Heat the oven to 180°C (350°F). Grease a baking dish.

5. Drain the chicken from the marinade and place in the baking dish. Spoon some marinade over the chicken and cook for 15–20 minutes, until the chicken is cooked.

6. Slice the chicken and place into the won ton shells. Garnish with the spring onion and coriander leaves.

Asian chicken with bean sprouts and red peppers

1. Heat the oil in a wok or a large frying pan until smoking, add the chicken and stir-fry for 4 minutes, stirring all the time. Remove the meat and set aside.

2. Add the spring onions, peppers and bamboo shoots and stir-fry for 3 minutes.

3. Mix the soy sauce with the cornflour and some water and stir into the vegetables.

4. Return the meat to the pan. Stir in the bean sprouts, cashew nuts, sesame oil and oyster sauce, and heat on a high flame for 30 seconds, then serve.

Preparation time: 15 min
Cooking time: 10 min
Serves 4

3 tbsp sunflower oil
4 chicken breasts, skinned and
* sliced into strips*
4 spring onions, chopped
2 red peppers, cut into strips
200g tinned bamboo shoots
5 tbsp soy sauce
2 tsp cornflour
150g bean sprouts
50g cashew nuts
1 tbsp sesame oil
2 tbsp oyster sauce

Steamed scallops

1. Open the scallops with a sharp knife and cut out the sphincter. Remove the top shell and remove the flesh and orange roe with a knife. Wash the flesh thoroughly several times.

2. Mix the flesh and roe with the lemon juice and season to taste with cayenne pepper, salt and pepper.

3. Place into the steamer basket. Place the peppers and spring onions on top. Pour the fish stock into the steamer and add the coriander stems and onion slices and bring to a boil. Cover the bamboo steamer and cook for 6 minutes.

4. Scatter with coriander leaves to garnish.

Preparation time: 10 min
Cooking time: 6 min
Serves 4

12 small scallops in shells
2 tbsp lemon juice
pinch cayenne pepper
½ red pepper, diced
½ green pepper, diced
½ yellow pepper, diced
2 spring onions, sliced
400ml fish stock
coriander stems, plus leaves to serve
1 onion, sliced

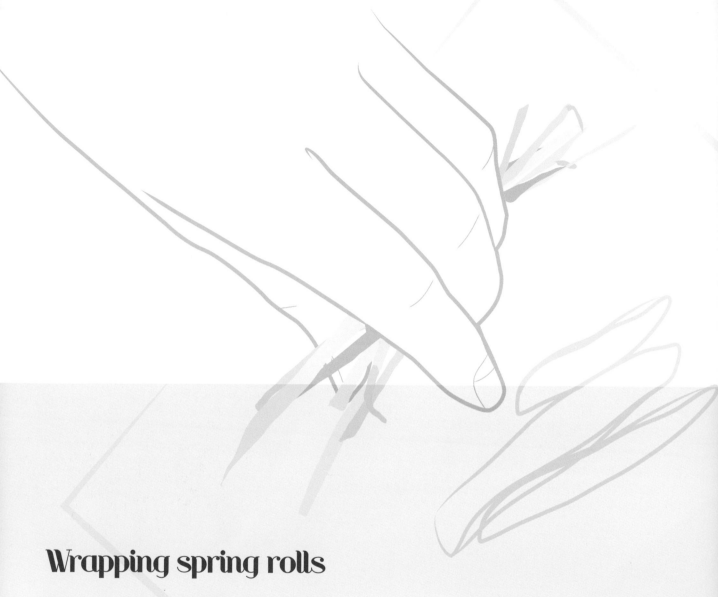

Wrapping spring rolls

These classic Asian accompaniments look impressive and when home-made taste so much better than shop-bought. The wrappers are widely available, so try this simple technique and chuck out the take-away menu.

STEP 1 Prepare the filling ingredients before starting on the spring rolls. Make sure the ingredients are thinly and evenly sliced to allow for smooth rolling.

STEP 2 Lay out a spring roll wrapper and brush the edges with egg white. Put some filling between the centre and one corner, and fold over to cover.

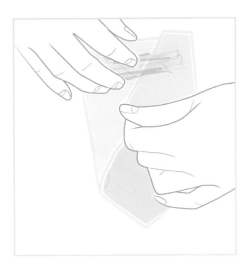

STEP 3 Fold in the sides of the spring roll wrapper over the covered filling, pressing one corner over the other as if making an envelope.

STEP 4 Using both hands, roll the filling end of the spring roll wrapper towards the unsealed end, keeping the roll tight as you go.

STEP 5 Roll up all the way along the wrapper until you reach the loose edge. Fold over the last corner, sticking it down with a little egg white.

Red perch curry with pineapple and cherry tomatoes

1. Drain the pineapple chunks and chop them. Reserve the juice.

2. Chop the fish into bite-size pieces. Remove any bones if found. Sprinkle lemon juice over the top and season to taste with salt and pepper.

3. Cook the rice according to the instructions on the pack.

4. Heat the oil in a wok or frying pan. Stir in the curry paste and cook briefly. Add the coconut milk and bring to a boil. Simmer for 2 minutes. Stir in the pineapple chunks.

5. Mix the yoghurt with the cornflour and add it to the wok.

6. Pour in some reserved pineapple juice and bring to a boil. Season with the soy sauce.

7. Add the fish pieces and the tomatoes and bring to a boil again. Cover, turn off the flame and allow to poach for 2–3 minutes. Stir in the basil.

8. Divide the rice equally into 4 lightly greased moulds. Turn the rice out of the moulds onto warmed plates. Serve the curry with the rice and garnish with chives.

Preparation time: 20 min
Cooking time: 30 min
Serves 4

For the fish curry:
1 (small) can pineapple chunks
500g perch fillet
2 tbsp lemon juice
200g basmati rice
1 tbsp peanut oil
1 tbsp red curry paste
400ml coconut milk
150ml yoghurt
1 tsp cornflour
1–2 tbsp light soy sauce
250g cherry tomatoes, halved
25g fresh basil, shredded

To garnish:
8 chives

Chinese spare ribs with rice

1. Place the ribs in a shallow baking dish.

2. Mix the soy sauce with the honey, hoisin sauce, rice vinegar, rice wine and garlic to make a marinade and add to the ribs, making sure they are well coated. Cover and marinate in the refrigerator for at least 6 hours.

3. Heat the oven to 180°C (350°F).

4. Cook for about 1 hour, brushing the ribs with the marinade from time to time.

5. Cook the rice according to the pack instructions, adding the peas during the last 10 minutes. Serve with the ribs.

Preparation time: 20 min
  plus 6 h marinating
Cooking time: 1 h
Serves 4

1kg pork ribs, cut into individual ribs
50ml soy sauce
2 tbsp honey
2 tbsp hoisin sauce
2 tbsp rice vinegar
2 tbsp rice wine
2 garlic cloves, finely chopped
250g long grain rice
200g frozen peas

Sichuan prawns in chilli sauce

1. Chop the fine black vein from the prawns, wash and dry on absorbent paper.

2. Heat the oil in a wok. Add the ginger, Sichuan pepper and garlic and spring onions and stir-fry for 30 seconds.

3. Add the prawns and stir-fry for 1 minute.

4. Add the tomato purée, chilli bean sauce, cider vinegar, sugar and sesame oil and stir-fry for another few minutes.

5. Place in bowls, garnished with coriander.

Preparation time: 10 min
Cooking time: 5 min
Serves 4

600g raw tiger prawns
1 tbsp groundnut oil
1 inch ginger, grated
1 tsp Sichuan pepper
2 garlic cloves, crushed
2 spring onions, trimmed and
  chopped
1 tbsp tomato purée
2 tsp chilli bean sauce
1 tsp cider vinegar
1 tsp sugar
2 tsp sesame oil
coriander leaves

Corn and crabmeat soup

Preparation time: 10 min
Cooking time: 10 min
Serves 4

1 egg white
1 tsp sesame oil
1 litre chicken stock
400g tinned sweetcorn, drained
1 tbsp rice wine
1 tbsp light soy sauce
1 inch ginger, grated
1 red chilli, finely chopped
1 tsp sugar
2 tsp cornflour
250g crabmeat, finely chopped
1 tbsp chopped coriander leaves
2 tbsp spring onions

1. Whisk together the egg white and sesame oil.

2. Bring the stock to a boil, add the sweetcorn and simmer for about 4 minutes.

3. Add the rice wine, soy sauce, ginger, chilli, a little salt and pepper and the sugar.

4. Grind the cornflour to a paste with 1 tablespoon cold water, stir into the soup and bring to a boil.

5. Add the chopped crab. Add the whisked egg white, stirring constantly, and season to taste with salt and pepper.

6. Ladle the soup into warmed bowls and scatter with the coriander and spring onions.

Egg noodle salad with sesame chicken and mangetout

1. Blanch the carrots and mangetout in salted boiling water for 3 minutes and drain. Rinse in cold water and drain well.

2. Cook the noodles according to the pack instructions, then drain, rinse in cold water and drain well.

3. Season the chicken with salt and pepper. Heat the oil in a frying pan and fry the chicken for 5 minutes on each side. Sprinkle with sesame seeds and toss a few times to coat on all sides. Remove from the pan and set aside.

4. Mix together the ginger, stock, soy sauce, vinegar, sambal oelek and sugar. Stir in the noodles and vegetables.

5. Divide between the serving bowls. Slice the chicken and place on top of the salad.

Preparation time: 15 min
Cooking time: 15 min
Serves 4

375g carrots, cut into sticks
200g mangetout, halved
200g egg noodles
550g chicken breast fillets
2 tbsp oil
2–3 tbsp sesame seeds
2 tsp freshly grated ginger
120ml vegetable stock
75ml soy sauce
2 tbsp white wine vinegar
1 tsp sambal oelek
pinch sugar

Lobster toasts with soy sauce

1. Toss the lobster meat in the cornflour.

2. Put the lobster, ginger, spring onions, soy sauce, sesame oil and egg white into a blender and blend to a coarse paste.

3. Spread the bread slices with the lobster paste, pressing the paste onto the bread. Cut each slice diagonally into 4 triangles.

4. Heat the rapeseed oil in a deep pan.

5. Dip the triangles in the whisked egg and fry in the oil, lobster side down, until golden brown.

6. Drain on kitchen paper and serve warm with a bowl of soy sauce for the dipping.

Preparation time: 10 min
Cooking time: 10 min
Serves 4

450g cooked lobster meat, cut into
  2cm pieces
3 tsp cornflour
2 tsp finely chopped ginger
5 spring onions, finely chopped
2 tbsp soy sauce
1 tsp sesame oil
1 egg white
4 slices white bread, crusts removed
250ml rapeseed oil
2 eggs, whisked

To serve:
soy sauce

Japanese noodle salad with salmon

1. Cook the noodles according to the instructions on the packet.

2. Blanch the courgettes and spring onions in boiling salted water for 3 minutes, then drain in a sieve. Drain the noodles as well.

3. Mix together the sesame oil, soy sauce, fruit vinegar, lemon juice, sugar, salt and cayenne pepper to taste.

4. Stir in the noodles, vegetables and salmon. Sprinkle with sesame seeds.

Preparation time: 10 min
Cooking time: 10 min
Serves 4

300g Japanese egg noodles
400g courgettes, cut into thin strips
125g spring onions, cut into thin strips
1 tbsp sesame oil
3 tbsp soy sauce
2 tbsp fruit vinegar
3 tbsp lemon juice
1 tsp sugar
cayenne pepper
250g very fresh salmon, thinly sliced
2 tsp black sesame seeds

Wasabi noodles with beans and tofu

Preparation time: 15 min
plus 30 min marinating
Cooking time: 50 min
Serves 4

400g tofu, diced
5–6 tbsp soy sauce
350g green Japanese buckwheat noodles
400g green beans (fresh or frozen)
2 tbsp sesame oil
2 tsp wasabi paste

1. Mix the tofu with the soy sauce. Marinate for 30 minutes, turning occasionally.

2. Cook the noodles and beans in salted boiling water until tender.

3. Heat the oil in a frying pan. Drain the tofu and cook until browned on all sides.

4. Drain the noodles and beans, mix with the wasabi paste and place on serving plates with the tofu.

Sweet and sour pork ragout with pineapple

1. Whisk the egg with the water and salt and marinate the meat for 15 minutes.

2. Mix together the Worcestershire sauce, soy sauce, vinegar, ketchup and sugar and set aside.

3. Take the meat out of the marinade, put into a bowl with 2 tablespoons cornflour and mix until coated.

4. Heat 3 tablespoons oil in a wok or frying pan and cook the pork for about 10 minutes, until cooked. Remove from the wok and set aside.

5. Heat the remaining oil in the wok and cook the pineapple and onion until lightly browned.

6. Add the prepared ketchup sauce to the wok and bring to a boil. Mix the remaining cornflour to a smooth paste with a little cold water, and stir into the sauce with the water. Boil for 1 minute.

7. Add the meat and reheat.

8. Spoon onto serving dishes and garnish with coriander leaves.

Preparation time: 10 min
 plus 15 min marinating
Cooking time: 20 min
Serves 4

1 egg
4 tbsp water
pinch salt
500g pork fillet, cut into bite–sized
* pieces*
1 tbsp Worcestershire sauce
1 tbsp soy sauce
2 tbsp rice vinegar
3 tbsp tomato ketchup
4 tbsp sugar
3 tbsp cornflour
4 tbsp oil
200g pineapple flesh, chopped
1 onion, diced
200–250 ml water

To garnish:
coriander leaves

Barbecued shrimp dumplings on lemon grass stalks

1. Place the red pepper, garlic and chillies into a small pan with some water, vinegar, lime juice and sugar. Bring to a boil and simmer gently for about 15 minutes to make the dipping sauce.

2. Place the shrimps in a bowl. Mix with the egg yolk, cornflour, fish sauce, sugar, sesame seeds and ground black pepper.

3. Divide the shrimp mixture into 8 portions and shape into chunky fingers around the lemon grass or wooden skewers.

4. Grill or fry over a medium flame until golden brown. Serve with the dipping sauce.

Preparation time: 10 min
Cooking time: 25 min
Serves 4

For the dip:
½ red pepper, diced
1 garlic clove, crushed
2 fresh red chillies, diced
175ml water
3 tbsp red wine vinegar
2 tbsp lime juice
1 tbsp sugar

For the shrimp cakes:
500g shrimps, chopped
1 egg yolk
1 tbsp cornflour
2 tbsp fish sauce
1 tsp sugar
1 tsp black sesame seeds
8 stalks lemon grass (or wooden skewers)

Rice noodle salad with shrimps

1. Cook the rice noodles according to the instructions on the packet.

2. Mix the curry paste with about 3 tablespoons of the hot noodle water until smooth. Stir in the fish sauce, sesame oil and lime juice.

3. Drain the rice noodles and cut into bite–sized pieces with scissors.

4. Put the rice noodles, shrimps, watercress and coriander leaves into a bowl. Add the curry paste mixture and mix well. Divide between serving bowls.

Preparation time: 10 min
Cooking time: 10 min
Serves 4

150g thin rice noodles
1 tsp green curry paste
1 ½ tbsp fish sauce
2 tbsp sesame oil
2 tbsp lime juice
300g cooked shrimps
1 bunch watercress leaves
1 bunch coriander leaves

Fried salmon fillet on pak choi

1. Cook the rice according to the pack instructions and keep warm.

2. Cut the pak choi in half lengthways and blanch in a large pan of salted boiling water for 3 minutes. Drain well and keep warm.

3. Mix the coriander with the sesame oil and lemon zest and juice and season with salt and pepper.

4. Heat the olive oil in a wide pan and cook the salmon skin side down over a high flame for 2 minutes, then turn it over and reduce the flame. Spread the coriander mixture over the top of the fish and continue cooking for 5 minutes or until the fish is just cooked through.

5. Put the rice and pak choi into serving bowls and arrange the salmon on top.

Preparation time: 15 min
Cooking time: 25 min
Serves 4

300g basmati rice
4 pak choi
25g fresh coriander, finely chopped
2 tbsp sesame oil
zest and juice of 2 limes
1 tbsp olive oil
4 salmon fillets

Coconut cream tart with rhubarb and raspberry compote

1. For the pastry: sift the flour into a mixing bowl and make a well in the centre. Scatter the icing sugar, vanilla and butter around the edge. Put the cream in the middle and quickly knead all ingredients to a dough. Form into a ball, wrapped in cling film and chill for 30 minutes. Heat the oven to 180°C (350°F). Grease a 26cm flan tin.

2. Roll the pastry out thinly on a floured surface and line the base and sides of the flan tin. Prick several times with a fork, covering with non-stick baking paper and baking beans and bake for about 20 minutes, until golden. Set aside to cool.

3. For the filling: mix together the soft cheese, coconut cream and coconut flakes. Whisk the egg whites until they form soft peaks and whisk in the sugar and salt until stiff. Fold into the cheese mixture and spread evenly in the cooled pastry case. Sprinkle with coconut flakes and chill until ready to serve with the rhubarb and raspberry compote.

4. For the compote: place the sugar, lemon juice and water into a pan and bring to a boil, stirring until the sugar has dissolved.

5. Add the rhubarb and simmer for about 3 minutes until tender. Turn the rhubarb, cover and leave to cool.

6. Stir the raspberries into the cooled rhubarb compote.

Preparation time: 25 min
  plus 30 min chilling
Cooking time: 25 min
Serves 4
For the pastry:
250g plain flour
50g icing sugar
1 tsp vanilla extract
125g butter
3 tbsp double cream
For the filling:
500g soft cream cheese
100g sweetened coconut cream
2 tbsp coconut flakes
2 egg whites
50g sugar
pinch salt
coconut flakes, for sprinkling
For the rhubarb and raspberry
  compote:
100g sugar
1 tsp lemon juice
150ml water
500g rhubarb, cut into 4cm pieces
150g raspberries

Pea soup with tempeh

1. Marinate the tempeh slices in the soy sauce.

2. Heat 3 tablespoons oil in a pan and cook the onion until transparent. Add the carrots, leek and potatoes and cook, stirring, for 5 minutes.

3. Pour in the stock, bring to a boil, add the peas and simmer for 20–30 minutes until the vegetables are tender. Season to taste with salt, pepper and nutmeg.

4. Heat the remaining oil in a frying pan and cook the tempeh on both sides until brown.

5. Ladle the pea soup into serving bowls and place the fried tempeh on top.

Preparation time: 15 min
Cooking time: 40 min
Serves 4

150g tempeh, sliced
2 tbsp soy sauce
5 tbsp oil
1 onion, finely chopped
2 carrots, thinly sliced
1 medium-sized leek, thinly sliced
200g potatoes, peeled and diced
1 litre vegetable stock
375g peas
grated nutmeg

Soya spring rolls with dip

1. Soak the glass noodles in hot water for 10 minutes. Drain and chop into smaller pieces using scissors.

2. Heat the sesame oil in a frying pan or wok. Add the soya mince and fry over a high flame, stirring, for about 2 minutes, until browned right through. Add the cabbage, carrot, garlic and glass noodles.

3. Season with sugar and soy sauce. Cook on a medium flame for a further 3 minutes. Set aside and leave to cool.

4. Spread out the spring roll wrappers. Place 2 tablespoons of the filling in the middle of each wrapper and roll up into rolls approximately 7cm long. Stick down the end of each roll with the whisked egg white.

5. Heat the oil to about 347°F in a pan or wok. Fry the spring rolls in batches for about 3 minutes, until golden brown. Drain on kitchen paper.

6. For the dip: purée the red pepper, garlic and chillies or crush in a mortar.

7. Put into a small pan with the water, vinegar and sugar and bring to a boil. Cook on a medium flame without a lid for about 30 minutes, until the sauce is slightly creamy. Check the seasoning.

8. Put the spring rolls on serving plates and serve the spicy dip separately.

Preparation time: 15 min
Cooking time: 45 min
Serves 20 spring rolls

100g glass noodles
2 tbsp sesame oil
250g soya mince
100g white cabbage, shredded
1 carrot, sliced into thin strips
2 garlic cloves, finely chopped
1 tbsp sugar
2–3 tbsp light soy sauce
20 spring roll wrappers, approx.
  20 x 20cm
1 egg white, whisked
1 litre vegetable oil, for deep-frying

For the dip:
1 red pepper, chopped
1 garlic clove, finely chopped
2 fresh red chillies, finely chopped
5 tbsp rice vinegar
75g sugar
250ml water

Pork curry with raisins

1. Soak the tamarind in the water.

2. Put the meat into a bowl with the fish sauce. Mix together and leave to stand for 10 minutes.

3. Heat the oil in a large frying pan and brown the meat on all sides in batches. Add the onions and fry until soft.

4. Add the bay leaf, peanuts and raisins and fry briefly. Stir in the coconut milk and stock, followed by the curry paste. Cover and simmer for 20 minutes.

5. Squeeze out the tamarind, discard the fibres and add the liquid to the curry.

6. Add the chilli and simmer for a further 15 minutes, until the meat is tender. Add salt and sugar to taste.

7. To garnish: strip the coriander leaves from their stalks and shred. Sprinkle over the curry.

Preparation time: 15 min
  plus 10 min standing
Cooking time: 50 min
Serves 4

1 tbsp pressed tamarind
125ml water
500g lean pork, cubed
50ml fish sauce
2 tbsp oil
2 onions, finely chopped
1 bay leaf
50g ground peanuts
2 tbsp raisins
400ml coconut milk
200ml vegetable stock
2 tbsp curry paste
1 red chilli
sugar, to taste

To garnish:
3–4 sprigs fresh coriander

Teriyaki beef fillet with chive tempura

1. Mix the cornflour with the baking powder and water.

2. Whisk the egg white until frothy and fold into the batter.

3. Heat the oil to 180°C (350°F).

4. Coat the chives and flowers in the batter and deep-fry in batches until crisp. Drain on kitchen paper.

5. For the beef fillet: mix the teriyaki sauce with the honey and sesame seeds and heat gently on a low flame. Add the pieces of beef fillet.

6. Heat the oil in a frying pan. Cook the beef pieces for 2–3 minutes on each side until cooked to your liking.

7. Put the meat on serving plates and arrange the chive and flower tempura on the meat. Garnish the plates with some wasabi oil.

Preparation time: 10 min
Cooking time: 15 min
Serves 4

For the chive tempura:
40g cornflour
½ tsp baking powder
40ml water
1 egg white
oil, for deep frying
8 chives
8 chive flowers

For the beef fillet:
3 tbsp teriyaki sauce
2 tbsp honey
2 tbsp sesame seeds
200–250 g beef fillet, in 4 pieces
2 tbsp oil

To garnish:
4 tbsp wasabi oil

Thai tomjuddang soup with stuffed cucumbers

Cooking time: 30 min
Serves 4

2 cucumbers, cut into 5cm pieces
400g minced meat
2 garlic cloves, finely chopped
2 coriander roots, chopped
soy sauce
800ml beef broth
fish sauce

To garnish:
coriander leaves

1. Scoop out the centres of the cucumber pieces.

2. Mix the meat with the garlic and the chopped coriander root.

3. Season to taste with soy sauce, salt and pepper. Stuff the cucumbers with the meat mixture.

4. Bring the beef broth to a boil. Add the cucumbers and cook for about 15–20 minutes until the meat is cooked.

5. Season with soy sauce and fish sauce, and garnish with coriander leaves.

Ginger cream with fruit

1. Soak the gelatine in a small bowl of cold water.

2. Whisk the egg yolks with the icing sugar and ginger syrup.

3. Heat the ginger ale, squeeze out the gelatine and dissolve in the warm ginger ale.

4. Mix a little of the egg yolk mixture with the gelatine. Gradually stir in the rest of the egg yolk mixture. Fold in the diced ginger and chill for 30 minutes until thick, but not set.

5. Whisk the cream until thick and fold into the ginger mixture. Divide between serving bowls and chill for 3 hours until set.

6. Decorate the ginger cream with the strips of fruit and the wafer biscuits.

Preparation time: 15 min
  plus 3 h 30 min chilling
Cooking time: 5 min
Serves 4–6

4 gelatine leaves
4 egg yolks
80g icing sugar
3–4 tbsp ginger syrup (from the
  ginger jar)
200ml ginger ale
4–6 pieces preserved ginger, diced
250ml double cream

To decorate:
papaya or mango, peeled and
  sliced into thin ribbons
6 wafer biscuits

Strips of beef with aubergine and beans

1. Marinate the meat with soy sauce and fish sauce.

2. Heat 3 tablespoons oil in a wok or frying pan and gently cook the beans, ginger, chilli and lemongrass.

3. Pour in the stock, bring to a boil and simmer for 5 minutes.

4. Add the aubergine and continue simmering.

5. Heat the remaining oil in another pan and brown the meat. Keep warm in a low oven.

6. Add the coriander to the vegetables, season with salt and pepper. Add the meat and heat through.

7. Place on serving plates and sprinkle with lime zest.

Preparation time: 30 min
Cooking time: 30 min
Serves 10

500g sirloin steak, cut into thin
  strips
3 tbsp dark soy sauce
1 tbsp fish sauce
5 tbsp sesame oil
500g green beans, sliced
40g ginger, finely chopped
1 red chilli, cut into strips
1 stalk lemongrass
150 –170 ml | 2/3 – 3/4 cup beef
  stock
2 aubergines (eggplants), peeled
  and diced
1 bunch coriander (cilantro),
  chopped
salt and pepper
1 tsp grated lime zest

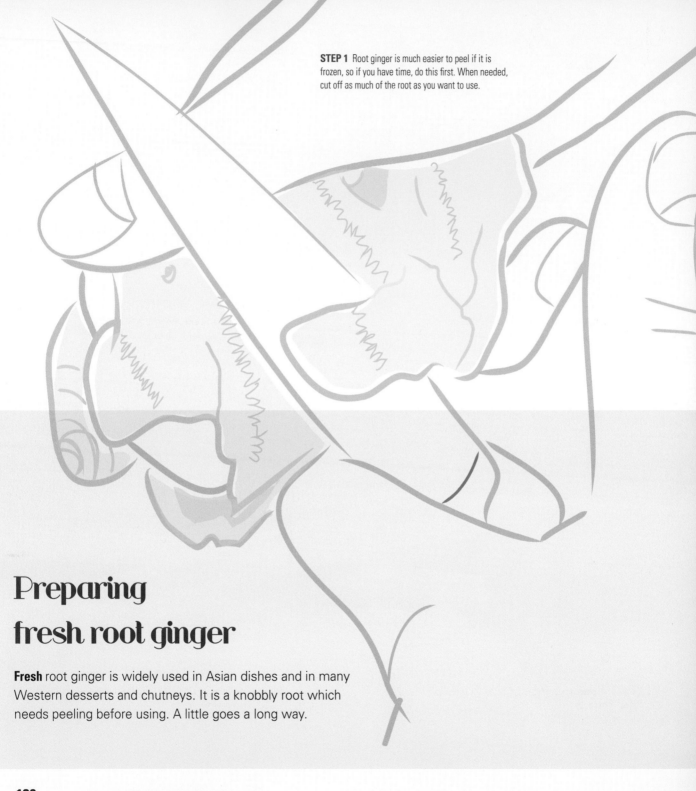

STEP 1 Root ginger is much easier to peel if it is frozen, so if you have time, do this first. When needed, cut off as much of the root as you want to use.

Preparing
fresh root ginger

Fresh root ginger is widely used in Asian dishes and in many Western desserts and chutneys. It is a knobbly root which needs peeling before using. A little goes a long way.

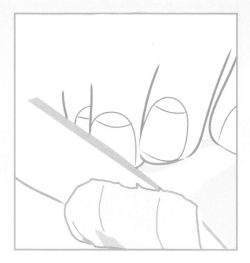

STEP 2 Using a sharp knife, carefully cut away the skin of the ginger root, taking care not to remove too much flesh at the same time.

STEP 3 Once the skin has been removed, carefully cut the chunk of ginger into thin slices with a large, heavy knife.

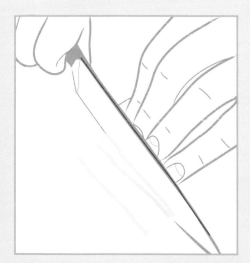

STEP 4 Cut the wide slices into smaller, thinner strips, similar in size to matchsticks.

STEP 5 Take the matchsticks of ginger and cut across them with a large knife to form tiny dice.

Fried cauliflower with saffron

1. Blanch the cauliflower in salted boiling water for 2–3 minutes. Drain.

2. Heat the ghee in a large frying pan. Fry the saffron, garlic, ginger, cumin and chillies for a few minutes. Add the cauliflower and fry gently for 10 minutes, stirring occasionally.

3. Season with salt and ground black pepper.

Preparation time: 10 min
Cooking time: 20 min
Serves 4

1 large cauliflower, divded into florets
4 tbsp ghee
pinch ground saffron
2 garlic cloves, finely chopped
4cm piece ginger, cut into thin strips
1 tsp ground cumin
2 green chilli peppers, deseeded, cut into fine strips

Beef with mushrooms

1. Cook the rice according to the pack instructions.

2. Blanch the mangetout in salted boiling water for 1 minute. Rinse in cold water and drain.

3. Heat the oil and quickly brown the meat. Add the mushrooms and fry briefly. Stir in the garlic and onions. Stir-fry all together for 1–2 minutes.

4. Add a little fish sauce, soy sauce and the stock. Add the mangetout and cook for 1–2 minutes. Season to taste with fish sauce, soy sauce and sesame oil.

5. Add the Thai basil leaves and sesame seeds.

6. Drain the rice and spoon onto serving plates and place the beef mixture on top.

Preparation time: 15 min
Cooking time: 20 min
Serves 4

200g long grain rice
250g mangetout
2 tbsp vegetable oil
600g beef, from the rump or sirloin,
  cut into thin strips
200g button mushrooms, halved
1 garlic clove, finely chopped
2 onions, sliced
100ml beef stock
fish sauce
soy sauce
1 tsp sesame oil
½ bunch Thai basil
1 tbsp sesame seeds

Chinese steamed pork buns

1. Dissolve the yeast in the lukewarm water. Add 125g flour and mix thoroughly. Cover with a cloth and leave to rise for 1 hour, until bubbles appear. Add the remaining flour to form a dough.

2. Knead the dough on a lightly floured surface until smooth. Place into a large, greased bowl in a warm place. Cover with a damp tea towel and leave to rise for about 2 hours until doubled in size.

3. For the filling: heat 2 tablespoons oil in a wok or frying pan. Stir-fry the spring onion and garlic for 30 seconds. Add the pork. Stir-fry for 1 minute. Add the soy sauce, oyster sauce and sugar.

4. Pour in the dissolved cornflour and stir quickly until the pork is glacéd. Remove from the pan and leave to cool.

5. On a floured board, knead the dough for 2 minutes. Cut into 24 pieces. Flatten each piece with the palm of your hand and roll with a rolling pin into 8cm rounds. Place 2 tablespoons of the filling on the centre of each round. Gather the dough up around the filling by pleating along the edges. Bring the pleats up and twist securely and firmly.

6. Place each bun on a 5cm square of non-stick baking paper on a steamer tray. Cover with a tea towel and leave to rise for 1 hour, until the dough springs back when touched with a finger. Remove the tea towel.

7. Steam the buns over briskly boiling water for 10 minutes.

Preparation time: 40 min
 plus 3 h rising
Cooking time: 15 min
Serves 24 buns

For the dough:
50g dried yeast or 1 cake
 fresh yeast
225ml lukewarm water
500g plain flour, plus extra for
 dusting
50g sugar
2 tbsp vegetable oil
110ml boiling water
2 tbsp sesame seed oil

For the filling:
2 tbsp oil
1 spring onion, finely chopped
1 garlic clove, finely chopped
225g cooked pork, diced
2 tbsp light soy sauce
2 tbsp oyster sauce
1 tbsp sugar
1 tbsp cornflour, dissolved in
 2 tbsp water

Chicken with chilli peppers and basil

Preparation time: 10 min
Cooking time: 10 min
Serves 4

3 tbsp sesame oil
4 boneless chicken breasts, cut
into bite-sized pieces
2 red chillies, cut into thin strips
2 shallots, sliced lengthways
fish sauce
light soy sauce

To garnish:
Thai basil leaves

1. Heat the oil in a wok or frying pan and brown the chicken on all sides.

2. Add the chillies and shallots and cook gently until the onion is translucent.

3. Add fish sauce and soy sauce to taste. Bring to a boil, stirring, until piping hot.

4. Divide between serving bowls and garnish with Thai basil leaves.

Samosas

1. For the pastry: mix together the flour, ghee, salt and water in a mixing bowl. Knead to a smooth dough. Cover and leave to rest for 20 minutes.

2. For the filling: blanch the broccoli and beans in salted boiling water for 4 minutes. Rinse in cold water and drain.

3. Heat the ghee in a frying pan and cook the cumin seeds for 1 minute. Add the ginger, chilli and ground spices and stir well.

4. Add the onion and cook gently for 4 minutes. Add the blanched vegetables and peas and cook for 3 minutes, stirring occasionally. Reducing the heat, cover and simmer for 5 minutes. Season with salt and leave to cool.

5. Divide the dough into 8 portions. Oil a large, wooden board and roll out each ball to a rectangle 20 x 10cm. Cut in half to form 2 squares.

6. Divide the filling between the dough squares and fold each wrapper diagonally in half to form a triangle. Press the edges down firmly.

7. Heat the oil in a large pan. Fry the samosas, a few at a time, in the hot oil for 3–4 minutes, turning once. Drain on kitchen paper.

Preparation time: 15 min
  plus 20 min resting
Cooking time: 30 min
Serves 4

For the pastry:
300g plain flour
4 tbsp ghee
1 tsp salt
175ml water

For the filling:
300g broccoli florets
100g green beans, finely chopped
3 tbsp ghee
½ tsp cumin seeds
2 tsp grated ginger
½ tsp chilli powder
1 tsp each, ground coriander, sweet
  paprika and garam masala
1 onion, finely chopped
125g peas
1 litre oil

Spicy pork vindaloo

1. Heat the oil in a frying pan. Brown the meat in batches. Return to the pan and add the onions, garlic and spices and cook for 2 minutes.

2. Pour in the lemon juice. Stir in the tamarind paste, sugar and water. Cover and simmer gently for 45–50 minutes. Add a little water if needed.

3. For the garnish: heat the oil and cook the potato slivers until golden. Drain on kitchen paper.

4. Season the curry and garnish with the potato slivers.

Preparation time: 20 min
Cooking time: 1 h
Serves 4

2 tbsp oil
800g pork, e.g. shoulder; diced
2 onions, finely chopped
2 garlic cloves, finely chopped
1 tsp ginger, freshly grated
½ tsp cumin
1 tsp mustard seeds
½ tsp curcuma
1 stick cinnamon
1 tbsp mustard oil
juice of 1 lemon
1 tsp tamarind paste
1 tsp brown sugar
150ml water

To garnish:
3 tbsp oil
1 new potato

Passion fruit and coconut cream

1. For the passion fruit cream: soak the gelatine in a small bowl of cold water. Chop the passion fruit in half. Scrape out the pulp with a spoon and press through a sieve (save 2 tablespoons of the seeds for the decoration).

2. Heat the rum until warm and add the squeezed-out gelatine until dissolved.

3. Mix the passion fruit pulp with the sugar and gelatine mixture.

4. Whisk the cream and egg white until stiff and fold into the passion fruit mixture. Spoon the cream into 4 glasses and chill.

5. For the coconut cream: soak the gelatine as before. Heat the coconut milk and sugar and bring to the boil. Remove from the flame.

6. Whisk the egg yolks until frothy and stir in the hot coconut milk gradually. Stir over a double boiler until creamy. Add the gelatine and stir until dissolved. Leave to cool. Add the lime juice.

7. Whisk the cream until stiff and fold in the coconut flakes. Carefully pour into the passion fruit cream. Chill for at least 3 hours before serving. Decorate with the reserved passion fruit seeds, lime slices, coconut slices and mango.

Preparation time: 25 min
  plus 3 h chilling
Cooking time: 5 min
Serves 3

For the passion fruit cream:
2 leaves gelatine
6 passion fruit
2 teaspoons white rum
100g sugar
100ml double cream
1 egg white

For the coconut cream:
2 leaves gelatine
150ml coconut milk
50g sugar
2 egg yolks
juice of ½ lime
100ml double cream
3 tbsp coconut flakes

To decorate:
lime slices
fresh coconut slices
mango pieces

Indonesian stir-fried noodles with shrimps and chicken

Preparation time: 15 min
Cooking time: 20 min
Serves 4

For the pancake mixture:
50g plain flour
1 egg
1 egg yolk
100ml milk
2 tbsp peanut oil

For the stir-fry noodles:
300g thin egg noodles
8 tbsp oil
500g boneless, skinless chicken
  breast fillets
6 spring onions, finely chopped
2 onions, finely chopped
3 garlic cloves, crushed
150g pak choi, quartered
2 red chilli peppers, finely sliced
1 tbsp fresh ginger, peeled and
  finely chopped
100g raw prawns
1 tsp sugar
2 tbsp light soy sauce
50ml vegetable broth

To garnish:
coriander leaves

1. For the pancakes: mix together the flour, egg, egg yolk, a pinch of salt and the milk into a blender.

2. Heat some oil in a frying pan, pour in a ladleful of the pancake batter and swirl to cover the base of the pan. Cook for 30 seconds until the base is firm. Turn over and cook for another 30 seconds. Place onto a plate and repeat with the rest of the batter.

3. Interleaving the pancakes with non-stick baking paper, wrap in foil and keep warm in a very low oven.

4. Cook the noodles in plenty of boiling, salted water according to the packet instructions and drain well.

5. Heat the oil in a wok or large frying pan and stir-fry the chicken for a few minutes until golden. Add the spring onions, onions and garlic and fry for 3 minutes.

6. Mix in the pak choi, chilli, ginger and the prawns and fry for 2 more minutes. Add salt and black pepper, sugar, soy sauce and broth. Mix in the noodles and heat through, stirring until warm.

7. Pile the noodles on to plates. Cut the pancakes into very thin strips and garnish on top with the coriander leaves.

Homemade paneer

1. Bring the milk slowly to a boil in a heavy-based pan, stirring.

2. Reducing the flame, add the lemon juice and salt. Stir gently until the white curd starts to form. Continue to stir gently, being careful not to break up the lumps. Remove from the flame.

3. Stir in the coriander and chilli flakes.

4. Pour the mixture through a colander lined with 4 layers of muslin. Tie up the muslin, then squeeze out as much liquid as you can. Hang the muslin bag over a bowl and let it continue to drip for about 1–1½ hours.

5. Place a heavy weight, such as a pan filled with water, on top of the wrapped cheese for 30 minutes.

Preparation time: 10 min
  plus 2 h standing
Cooking time: 10 min
Serves 4

2 litres whole milk
60ml lemon juice
pinch salt
4 tbsp chopped coriander leaves
1 tsp dried red chilli flakes

Prawn laksa

1. For the curry paste: mix together all the ingredients in a blender and blend to a smooth paste.

2. Heat the oil in a frying pan and cook the tofu until golden brown. Remove and set aside.

3. Mix the fish stock with the shrimp and curry pastes. Place into a pan and bring to a boil. Reducing the heat, add the coconut milk, prawns, spring onions and tofu. Simmer gently for 2 minutes.

4. Add the beansprouts and simmer for a further 1–2 minutes. Stir in the coriander.

5. Cook the glass noodles according to the instructions on the pack. Drain and divide between 4 soup bowls while still hot.

6. Ladle the soup over the noodles and garnish with coriander.

Preparation time: 10 min
Cooking time: 10 min
Serves 4

For the curry paste:
1 shallot, finely chopped
2 garlic cloves, finely chopped
3cm piece ginger, finely chopped
1–2 stalks lemongrass, finely
  chopped
1 tbsp fish sauce
1 tbsp sambal oelek
1–2 tbsp lime juice
1 tsp ground cumin

For the soup:
2 tbsp oil
150g tofu, diced
750ml fish stock
1 tsp shrimp paste
350ml coconut milk
400g prawns
4 spring onions, diced
250g beansprouts
bunch coriander leaves, chopped
100g glass noodles

To garnish:
coriander leaves

Deep-fried lentil balls with peanut dip

1. For the lentil balls: Place the lentils and stock in a pan. Bring to the boil, cover and cook for about 15 minutes until soft. The liquid should be absorbed completely. Remove from the heat and set aside.

2. Mix the lentils with the egg, spring onion, garlic and herbs in a blender and purée. Mix in breadcrumbs until mouldable. Season with cumin, salt and cayenne pepper and form into balls.

3. Heat the oil in a deep pan and fry the balls in batches for 1–2 minutes until golden brown. Drain on kitchen paper.

4. For the dip: heat the oil and fry the garlic until soft.

5. Stir in the peanut butter and coconut milk and bring to a boil. Cook until thickened and reduced to the desired consistency. Season with cayenne pepper and soy sauce and pour into a small bowl.

Preparation time: 15 min
Cooking time: 20 min
Serves 4

For the lentil balls:
250g red lentils
200ml vegetable stock
1 egg
1 spring onion, chopped
1 garlic clove, finely chopped
½ bunch parsley, chopped
½ bunch coriander, chopped
breadcrumbs, as needed
ground cumin
cayenne pepper
oil, for deep frying

For the dip:
1 tbsp peanut oil
1 garlic clove, chopped
3 tbsp peanut butter
200ml coconut milk
cayenne pepper
soy sauce

Naan bread with mango chutney

1. Warm the milk and pour into a bowl. Crumble the yeast over the top and add 1 teaspoon sugar. Stir until dissolved and leave for 15 minutes until frothy.

2. Sift the flour into a mixing bowl, add the salt and baking powder and mix to combine. Add 1 teaspoon sugar, the milk and yeast mixture, oil, yoghurt and egg and knead to form a smooth dough.

3. Shape into a ball and return to the bowl. Cover with cling film and leave in a warm place to rise for 1 hour.

4. Heat the oven to 240°C (475°F). Grease a baking tray.

5. Knead the dough again, together with the chopped coriander and divide into 4 pieces. Roll into balls, and roll out the balls on a floured surface to a naan shape. Place on the baking tray and bake for about 8 minutes until golden brown.

6. For the mango chutney: mix all ingredients together with 3–4 tablespoons water. Bring to a boil, stirring and simmer for 10–15 minutes, until the mango is soft. Season to taste with salt and pepper and leave to cool. Remove the bay leaf, cloves and cinnamon stick.

Preparation time: 25 min
  plus 1 h 15 min rising and standing
Cooking time: 30 min
Serves 4

For the naan bread:
75ml milk
10g fresh yeast
2 tsp sugar
250g plain flour
½ tsp salt
½ tsp baking powder
1 tbsp oil
75ml plain yoghurt
1 small egg, whisked
2–3 tbsp chopped coriander

For the mango chutney:
200g mango, peeled and diced
2 tbsp sultanas
1 ½ tbsp brown sugar
1–2 tbsp red wine vinegar
1 stick cinnamon
2 cloves
1 bay leaf
1 tbsp paprika

Pickled Asian vegetables

1. Cover the vegetables and plums with boiling water and stand for 1 minute. Drain.

2. Mix together the garlic, spices, salt, sugar, vinegar and water. Pour over the vegetables in a pan.

3. Bring to a boil and cook for 10 minutes. Cool, cover and leave to pickle for 24 hours before serving.

Preparation time: 10 min
    plus 24 h pickling
Cooking time: 10 min
Serves 4

3 red peppers, quartered
2 onions, quartered
4 yellow plums
3 garlic cloves, crushed
1 ½ tsp turmeric
½ tsp chilli powder
2 tsp grated ginger
2 tsp salt
2 tbsp sugar
600ml white vinegar
200ml water

Thai mangosteen-clam curry

Preparation time: 15 min
Cooking time: 15 min
Serves 4

6 tbsp olive oil
3–4 garlic cloves, finely chopped
2 red chillies, cut into strips
1kg fresh clams, or mixed shellfish
250ml water
125ml fish stock
1–2 tbsp lime juice
5 tbsp chopped Thai basil
1 mangosteen, puréed

To garnish:
1 red chilli, cut into thin strips
¼ bunch chives
6–8 kaffir lime leaves

1. Heat 4 tablespoons oil in a frying pan. Cook the garlic and chillies until soft, without browning.

2. Add the clams and heat for 3 minutes, until all the shells have opened.

3. Add the water, fish stock and lime juice and cook on a low flame for 4 minutes.

4. Put the clams into a bowl and strain the liquid through a fine sieve, to remove any last traces of sand. Return the clams to the liquid, add the Thai basil and the remaining olive oil and season well with pepper and some salt.

5. Mix the mango purée with a little of the clam cooking liquid and heat through.

6. Spoon the mangosteen purée into serving bowls. Add the clams and garnish with chilli, chives and lime leaves.

Thai-style pork chop with broccoli

1. Place the chops in a shallow dish.

2. Mix together the soy sauce, water, garlic, pepper and ginger and pour over the chops. Marinate for at least 4 hours. Drain the chops, discarding the marinade.

3. Heat the grill.

4. Grill the onion slices and chops for 4–6 minutes on each side until cooked.

5. Cook the broccoli in salted boiling water for 4–5 minutes.

6. Mix together the remaining ingredients in a blender until almost smooth. Serve with the broccoli and chops. Garnish with coriander.

Preparation time: 15 min
  plus 4 h marinating
Cooking time: 15 min
Serves 4

4 boneless pork chops
60ml soy sauce
60ml water
1 garlic clove, crushed
1 tsp pepper
½ tsp grated ginger
1 red onion, sliced
250g broccoli florets
2 garlic cloves
1 red chilli, finely sliced
2 tbsp vegetable oil
2 tbsp lime juice
2 tbsp soy sauce
1 tsp Thai fish sauce
chopped coriander leaves

Spicy Indian pilau with carrots, apricots and raisins

1. Heat the butter in a frying pan and cook the onion until soft. Add the cardamom pods, cinnamon stick and the cloves and continue to fry for 2–3 minutes.

2. Add the rice and fry until transparent. Pour in the water. Dissolve the saffron in the hot water, season with pepper and add to the rice mixture.

3. Add the carrot, 2 tablespoons almonds, the raisins and the apricots. Bring to a boil and simmer for 40 minutes on a low flame.

4. Season with sea salt and serve, garnished with the remaining chopped almonds.

Preparation time: 15 min
Cooking time: 50 min
Serves 4

1 tbsp butter
1 onion, peeled and chopped
2 cardamom pods, halved
1 stick cinnamon
4 cloves
300g basmati rice
700ml water
½ tsp saffron threads
1 tbsp hot water
½ tsp pepper
1 large carrot, cut into thin sticks
4 tbsp almonds, or cashew nuts, chopped
4 tbsp raisins
5 dried apricots, sliced into strips

Chinese rice pudding

1. Wash the sticky rice in a sieve. Place into a bowl and steam in a bamboo steamer for 30 minutes. Mix the cooked rice with half the sugar.

2. Grease 4 small moulds, or 1 large mould.

3. Mix together all the diced candied fruits, lotus seeds, raisins, peach kernels and watermelon seeds.

4. Distribute the mixed fruit evenly around the sides of the moulds. Place the rice in the middle and press into the moulds so that they are filled evenly, right to the edges.

5. Place the moulds in the bamboo steaming basket and steam for 15 minutes. Turn out carefully onto serving plates.

6. Place the remaining sugar into a frying pan with the water and bring to a boil. Slowly add the mixed cornflour paste and boil until the syrup thickens. Pour over the pudding.

Preparation time: 15 min
Cooking time: 50 min
Serves 4

150g sticky rice
200g sugar
4 candied dates, finely diced
2 green Chinese pickled candied
   plums, finely diced
4 pieces candied winter melon,
   finely diced
4 dried longan fruits, finely diced
10g cooked lotus seeds
2 tbsp raisins
10 peach kernels
handful watermelon seeds
250ml water
1–2 tbsp cornflour, mixed with a
   little water

Lentil curry with paneer

Preparation time: 10 min
Cooking time: 25 min
Serves 4

2 tbsp butter
2 onions, finely chopped
2 garlic cloves, finely chopped
1 tsp turmeric
1 pinch ground cloves
1 pinch ground cumin
1 pinch ground allspice
2 curry leaves
250ml coconut milk
400ml vegetable stock
200g black lentils
200g red lentils
200g paneer, diced

1. Heat the butter and gently cook the onions and garlic until soft. Add the spices and cook for 1 minute.

2. Add the coconut milk, a little stock and the black lentils. Cover and simmer gently for 10 minutes.

3. Add the red lentils and some more stock. Simmer for a further 10 minutes, stirring occasionally, adding the remaining stock as necessary.

4. Remove the curry leaves and season to taste with salt and pepper. Stir in the paneer.

Chicken kerala

1. Heat the oil in a large frying pan and gently fry the red onions until crisp, but not burnt. Remove from the pan and set aside.

2. Fry the curry leaves for 2 minutes then set aside.

3. Fry the white onion gently until soft but not brown. Add the garlic, ginger, turmeric, garam masala, chilli peppers, mustard seeds, coriander seeds, cloves, peppercorns and salt.

4. Fry the mixture for 2 minutes, then add the chicken. Stir briefly. Pour in the chicken stock and coconut milk. Simmer gently, stirring from time to time, for 20 minutes or until the chicken is cooked through.

5. Scatter the red onions over the chicken and garnish with the curry leaves.

Preparation time: 15 min
Cooking time: 30 min
Serves 4

6 tbsp oil
2 red onions, finely sliced
16 curry leaves
1 white onion, finely chopped
2 garlic cloves, chopped
thumb-size piece ginger, finely chopped
1 tsp turmeric
1 tsp garam masala
2 red chilli peppers, finely chopped
1 tsp mustard seeds, crushed
1 tsp coriander seeds, crushed
4 cloves, crushed
1 tsp peppercorns, crushed
1 tsp salt
4 chicken breasts, skinned and cut into chunks
125ml chicken stock
125ml coconut milk

Chicken satay with ginger-coconut sauce

1. Mix together the chicken, 2 tablespoons oil and the spice mixture. Cover and chill.

2. Heat the remaining oil in a frying pan and gently cook the shallots and garlic without browning.

3. Stir in the ginger and chillies, then stir in the white wine. Add the coconut milk, honey and creme fraiche and simmer, stirring occasionally, to produce a creamy sauce.

4. Strain through a sieve, add the coriander and add fish sauce to taste.

5. Thread the chicken onto skewers and fry or grill for 5–6 minutes, turning frequently.

Preparation time: 10 min
Cooking time: 30 min
Serves 4

4 chicken legs, meat skinned and diced
3 tbsp peanut oil
1 tsp spice mixture, (equal parts ground ginger, black and white pepper, cayenne pepper)
3 shallots, finely chopped
2 garlic cloves, finely chopped
1 tsp grated ginger
2 chillies, finely chopped
150ml white wine
250ml coconut milk
1 tbsp honey
125ml creme fraiche
2 tbsp chopped coriander leaves
1 tbsp fish sauce

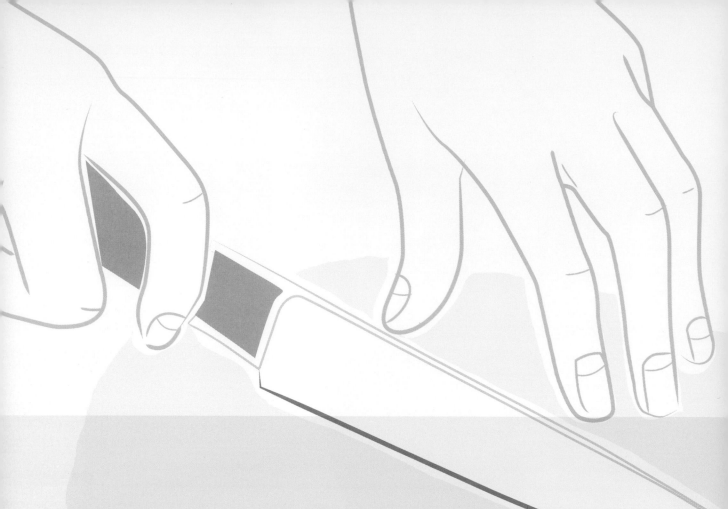

Making samosas

These delicious Asian parcels are surprisingly easy to make and can be eaten as a snack or alongside other Asian dishes. The filling can be made from any ingredient you wish, to suit any diet, taste or mood!

STEP 1 Divide the samosa dough into even pieces and roll each into a ball. On a large board or work surface, roll out until thin, then cut each into two semi-circles.

STEP 2 Taking one semi-circle at a time, place a teaspoonful of filling in the centre of the pastry, just in from the edge.

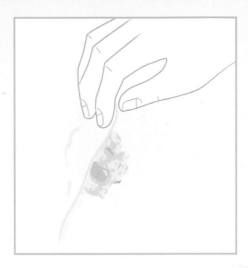

STEP 3 Using your hands, fold over one side of the pastry to cover and seal in the filling and to form a neat triangle shape.

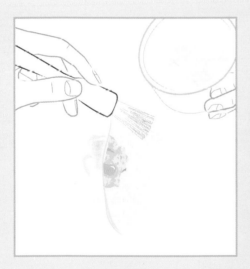

STEP 4 Using a pastry brush, paint the exposed edges of the pastry with a little beaten egg.

STEP 5 Fold over the remaining pastry portion to cover the filling completely, then press along the edges to seal.

Honey and soy glazed sesame tofu

1. Peel the limes with a very sharp knife and chop the peel into strips. Squeeze the juice from the fruit.

2. Whisk together the honey, soy sauce, lime juice and sesame oil. Mix with the tofu and leave to marinate for 2 hours.

3. Heat the grill. Thread the tofu onto wooden skewers. Grill the kebabs for about 2 minutes on each side, turning and basting as they cook.

4. Sprinkle the sesame seeds and garnish with lime curls.

Preparation time: 10 min
  plus 2 h marinating
Cooking time: 5 min
Serves 4

2 limes
2 tbsp honey
2 tbsp soy sauce
2 tbsp sesame oil
400g firm tofu, cubed
1 tbsp sesame seeds

Mango rice pudding

1. Place the rice, milk, cream and saffron threads in a pan and bring to the boil. Cover and simmer for 10 minutes.

2. Stir in the sugar, pistachios, almonds, raisins, rosewater and cardamom. Cover and cook the rice for a further 10 minutes.

3. Add the mango to the rice.

Preparation time: 10 min
Cooking time: 20 min
Serves 4

140g basmati rice
400ml milk
50ml double cream
6 saffron threads
60g brown sugar
25g pistachios, chopped
50g flaked almonds
1 tbsp raisins
1 tsp rosewater
pinch ground cardamom
1 mango, diced

Sushi rolls with soy sauce

1. For the sushi rice: wash the rice in a sieve until the water runs clear. Drain the rice briefly, then place into a pan with the water and bring to the boil. Cover and cook very gently on a very low flame for about 25 minutes, putting a towel between the pan and the lid.

2. For the rice marinade, place the vinegar, sugar, salt and seaweed into a pan. Bring to the boil and strain. Transfer the rice to a bowl and stir in the marinade. Quickly toast the nori sheets in a dry frying pan.

3. Mix together the vinegar and water and use to moisten your hands as you work.

4. Put 1 nori sheet on a bamboo mat and spread quarter of the rice on top, leaving approximately 2cm free at the upper edge.

5. Press the rice flat and spread a line of wasabi approximately 1cm wide horizontally across the middle. Lay a quarter of the lettuce, cucumber and salmon on the lower quarter of the rice. Roll up firmly, using the bamboo mat.

6. Wet your hands with vinegar water and mould the roll into a perfect shape. Dip a sharp knife into the vinegar water and cut the rolls in half at an angle. Make 3 more rolls in the same way using the rest of the ingredients.

7. Place the rolls on a serving plate and the soy sauce in a small dish.

Preparation time: 15 min
Cooking time: 30 min
Serves 4

For the sushi rice:
250g sushi rice
250ml water
2 tbsp rice vinegar
1 tbsp sugar
1 tsp salt
1 small piece seaweed

For the rolls:
4 nori sheets
4 tbsp vinegar
1 tbsp water
500g cooked sushi rice
wasabi
8 oak leaf lettuce leaves, torn
½ cucumber, cut into strips
400g salmon, cut into strips

To serve:
soy sauce

Palak paneer

Preparation time: 10 min
Cooking time: 20 min
Serves 4

4 tbsp butter
400g paneer, diced
2 onions, finely chopped
2 garlic cloves, finely chopped
1 tsp grated ginger
½ tsp ground coriander
½ tsp ground turmeric
½ tsp ground cumin
½ tsp chilli powder
1kg spinach, chopped
150ml double cream

1. Heat 2 tablespoons butter in a frying pan and fry the paneer until golden brown. Remove and set aside.

2. Heat the remaining butter in the pan and cook the onions, garlic and ginger until golden brown.

3. Stir in the spices, then add the spinach. Cover and cook gently for 10 minutes.

4. Add most of the cream (reserve 4 tablespoons) and the paneer. Simmer for a further 5 minutes.

5. Season to taste with salt and serve drizzled with the rest of the cream.

Pork stir-fry in lettuce cups

1. Mix together the fish sauce, 1 tablespoon oil and half the chilli strips. Add the meat and stir well. Cover and leave to marinate for 30 minutes.

2. Cook the noodles according to the pack instructions. Drain well and set aside.

3. Heat 2 tablespoons oil in a wok or frying pan. Add the meat (reserve the marinade) and stir fry for 1 minute until browned. Remove and set aside.

4. Add the remaining chilli strips, garlic, leeks and mushrooms and stir fry for 1–2 minutes.

5. Stir in the meat, marinade and sugar and cook for 3 minutes. Stir in the noodles.

6. Spoon into lettuce leaves just before serving.

Preparation time: 10 min
  plus 30 min marinating
Cooking time: 10 min
Serves 4

2 tbsp fish sauce
3 tbsp vegetable oil
1 green chilli, cut into strips
400g pork fillet, thinly sliced
350g thin Asian egg noodles
2 garlic cloves, finely chopped
1 leek, cut into thin strips
150g shiitake mushrooms, sliced
1 tsp sugar
1 lettuce

Coconut fish curry

1. Place the garlic, ginger, coconut milk, sesame oil, soy sauce, chilli powder, lemon juice and almonds into a blender and process until smooth. Stir in the vegetable stock.

2. Place into a wok or frying pan. Add the spring onions and peas and bring to the boil. Reducing the flame, simmer gently for 4 minutes. Season to taste with salt and pepper.

3. Add the fish and cook very gently for 4–5 minutes.

4. Pour into serving bowls and garnish with basil and coriander.

Preparation time: 10 min
Cooking time: 10 min
Serves 4

3 garlic cloves
1 walnut-sized piece of ginger
200ml coconut milk
5 tbsp sesame oil
5 tbsp light soy sauce
½ tsp chilli powder
2 tbsp lemon juice
2 tbsp chopped almonds
500ml vegetable stock
½ bunch spring onions, sliced
100g peas
600g fish fillet, (e. g. cod or redfish); diced

To garnish:
basil leaves
coriander leaves

Steamed salmon fillet with garlic oil

1. Season the salmon fillets with salt and pepper and drizzle with lime juice.

2. Heat the sesame oil and gently fry the garlic. As soon as the garlic begins to colour, remove from the flame and stir in the spring onions.

3. Place the salmon in a steamer. Bring the water to the boil in a suitable pan and insert the steamer. Cover and steam the fish for about 7 minutes, until cooked.

4. Arrange the salmon on serving plates and dress with the garlic oil and spring onions.

Preparation time: 10 min
Cooking time: 10 min
Serves 4

4 salmon fillets with skin (each around 200g), rinsed and dried
juice of 1 lime
4 tbsp light sesame oil
8 garlic cloves, finely chopped
2 spring onions, chopped into 5cm strips

Chicken curry with peas

Preparation time: 10 min
Cooking time: 15 min
Serves 4

200g basmati rice
750g chicken breast fillets, cut
  into bite sized pieces
2 tsp cornflour
salt and pepper to taste
2 tbsp oil
1 onion, diced
2 garlic cloves, finely chopped
1 red chilli, finely chopped
250ml coconut milk
2 tbsp red curry paste
1 tsp sugar
1 tbsp fish sauce
3–4 tbsp lemon juice
250g peas

To garnish:
coriander leaves

1. Cook the basmati rice according to the pack instructions.

2. Toss the chicken in the cornflour and season to taste with salt and pepper.

3. Heat the oil in a wok or frying pan and quickly brown the chicken pieces. Add the onion, garlic and chilli and cook for 5 minutes.

4. Stir in the coconut milk, curry paste, sugar and fish sauce. Cover and cook over a low heat for about 5–6 minutes until well blended. Stir in lemon juice to taste.

5. Stir in the peas and simmer for a further 3 minutes.

6. Drain the rice and divide between serving bowls. Spoon the curry on top and garnish with coriander.

Lamb biryani with almonds

1. Heat 4 tablespoons butter in a pan and cook half the onions until translucent. Add the ginger, cardamom, garlic, cloves, cinnamon and meat and fry, stirring, until the meat is lightly browned on all sides.

2. Stir in the ground spices, yoghurt and stock and season to taste with salt. Cover and simmer over a low heat for 45–60 minutes, stirring occasionally (it will be very thick).

3. Cook the remaining onions in another pan without letting them colour.

4. Wash the rice in a sieve under running water and add it to the onions with just double the amount of lightly salted water. Bring to a boil and cook, covered, over a very low heat for about 5 minutes.

5. Heat the oven to 180°C (350°F). Grease a baking dish.

6. Place the meat into the baking dish.

7. Drain the rice and mix with the raisins. Heat the milk, add the saffron and 2 tablespoons butter and stir well. Add the milk to the rice and mix with the meat in the dish. Cover and cook for about 1 hour, until the meat is tender.

8. Lightly toast the almonds in the remaining butter.

9. Fluff up the lamb biryani with a fork. Season to taste and spoon onto plates. Sprinkle with coriander to garnish.

Preparation time: 20 min
Cooking time: 2 h 10 min

7 tbsp butter
2 onions, diced
2 tsp grated ginger
6 cardamom pods
3 garlic cloves, crushed
5 cloves
1 cinnamon stick, broken
650g lamb, cut into bite-sized pieces
½ tsp ground cumin
½ tsp turmeric
1 pinch chilli powder
150ml plain yoghurt
150ml meat stock
300g basmati rice
50g raisins
4 tbsp milk
few saffron threads
6 tbsp blanched almonds
coriander leaves

Potato pakoras with yoghurt sauce

1. Cook the potatoes in salted boiling water for 30 minutes or until soft and then mash.

2. Mix the gram flour, cornmeal and the fennel seeds in a bowl. Stir in the chillies, coriander and onion. Add the potatoes and as much water as necessary to form a thick, kneadable dough.

3. Heat the oil in a deep frying pan until bubbles appear on a wooden spoon held in the fat.

4. Drop teaspoon-sized portions of the dough into the oil and fry until golden yellow. Drain on kitchen paper.

5. For the yoghurt sauce: mix all the ingredients together and season to taste.

Preparation time: 25 min
Cooking time: 45 min
Serves 4

450g potatoes, peeled and cut into
    chunks
75g gram flour
50g cornmeal
1 tsp fennel seeds
3 green chilli peppers, finely chopped
2 tbsp chopped coriander leaves
1 onion, finely chopped
sunflower oil, for frying

For the yoghurt sauce:
250ml yoghurt
1 tsp sugar
pinch salt
1 tbsp chopped coriander leaves
1 tbsp chopped mint leaves

Preparing scallops

You can buy scallops already opened and prepared, but if you fancy serving them in their own shell, you will have to open them up yourself. It's easy to do when you know how!

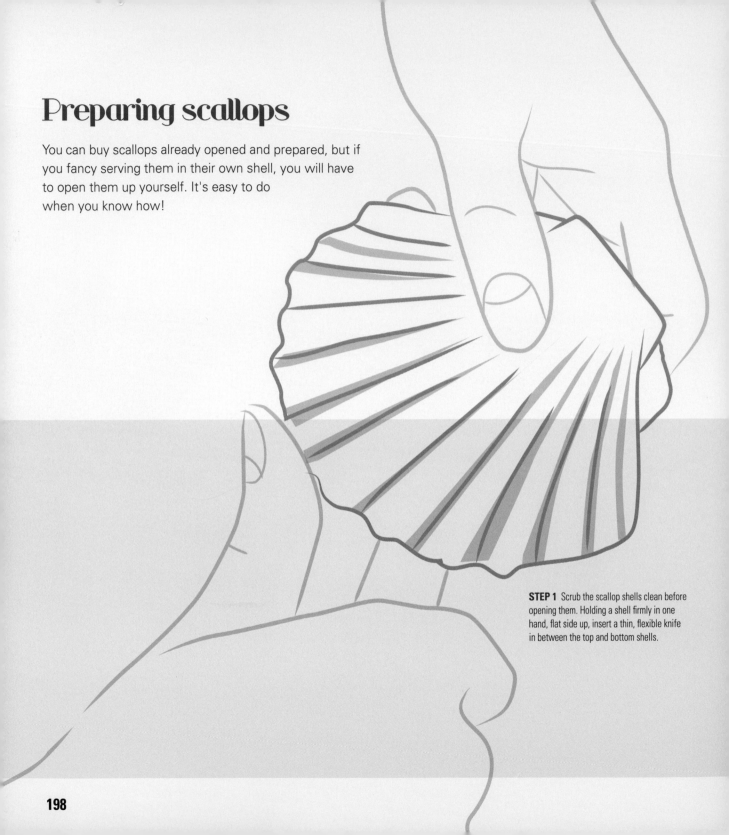

STEP 1 Scrub the scallop shells clean before opening them. Holding a shell firmly in one hand, flat side up, insert a thin, flexible knife in between the top and bottom shells.

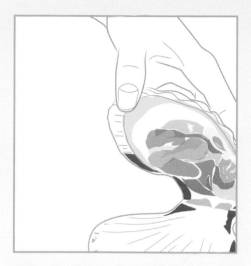

STEP 2 Keeping the knife blade close to the top shell, to avoid damaging the scallop, prise open the two shells carefully.

STEP 3 Slide the knife around the top shell to gently loosen the scallop, remove the bottom shell and detach the scallop from the shell with a knife.

STEP 4 Pull away the viscera and the frilly membrane and discard, then remove the black piece by the scallop.

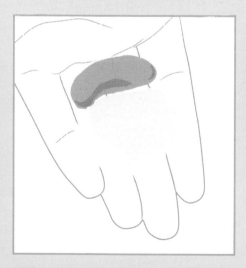

STEP 5 Separate out the scallop and its pinky coral and rinse both well. Pat dry with kitchen paper before cooking.

Chicken tikka

1. Mix together the garlic, ginger, sesame oil, lime juice, yoghurt and tomato purée. Stir in the cardamom, coriander, cumin, turmeric, chilli and cloves.

2. Add the chicken. Cover and marinate in the refrigerator for at least 4 hours.

3. Cover a grill pan with foil. Remove the chicken from the marinade. Place on the grill pan and grill for 3 minutes until the meat is just brown. Turn and grill for a further 3–5 minutes.

4. Season with salt and serve with the lime slices.

Preparation time: 15 min
  plus 4 h marinating
Cooking time: 10 min
Serves 4

2 garlic cloves, crushed
1 walnut-sized piece ginger,
  grated
4 tbsp sesame oil
4 tbsp lime juice
2 tbsp yoghurt
½ tbsp tomato purée
½ tsp ground cardamom
1 tsp ground coriander
1 tsp ground cumin
½ tsp turmeric
1 tsp chilli powder
1 pinch ground cloves
4 chicken breasts, skinned and
  cut into 1cm strips
lime slices

Minced lamb with peas

1. Heat the oil in a frying pan and add the bay leaves, peppercorns and onions. Fry, stirring often, until the onions are golden.

2. Add the ginger and garlic and fry, stirring, for 1–2 minutes.

3. Mix in the tomato purée and fry until the oil separates.

4. Add the lamb, peas, chilli, turmeric, garam masala and salt. Cover and cook on a low flame for about 25 minutes, stirring now and then.

Preparation time: 15 min
Cooking time: 30 min
Serves 4

6 tbsp oil
2 bay leaves
10 black peppercorns
2 onions, finely chopped
2 tsp grated ginger
2 tsp grated garlic
8 tbsp tomato purée
300g minced lamb
150g peas
1 tsp chilli powder
1 tsp turmeric
1 tsp garam masala

Fried rice triangles

1. Place the glutinous and Japanese rice in a bowl and wash with cold water. Drain the rice in a colander and set aside for 30 minutes.

2. Place the rice in a pan and add the water. Soak for 30 minutes. Bring to a boil and cook for 15–20 minutes until the rice is tender. When the rice is cooked, let it steam for 15 minutes.

3. Mash the rice until sticky. With wet hands, shape the rice into triangles.

4. Mix the pine nuts and sugar and coat the triangles in the pine nuts and sugar on both sides.

5. Heat the oil in a frying pan and fry the rice triangles until golden on both sides.

Preparation time: 20 min
  plus 1 h soaking
Cooking time: 30 min
Serves 4

300g glutinous rice
65g Japanese rice
350ml water
200g pine nuts
4 tbsp sugar
4 tbsp oil

Beef vindaloo

Preparation time: 15 min
  plus 2 h marinating
Cooking time: 2 h
Serves 4

2 cloves, ground
1 cinnamon stick
½ tsp cardamom seeds
1 tsp cumin seeds
1 tsp coriander seeds
50ml malt vinegar
800g beef, chopped into
  bite-sized chunks
2 tbsp ghee
2 onions, diced
4 garlic cloves, chopped
1 walnut-sized piece ginger, grated
2 red chillies, chopped
200g tinned tomatoes, chopped
600ml beef stock
1 tsp brown sugar
1 tsp peppercorns, crushed
2 tsp lime juice
parsley leaves

1. Finely grind the cloves, cinnamon, cardamom, cumin and coriander in a mortar. Add the vinegar and pour the mixture over the meat in a bowl. Mix well, cover and leave to marinade for about 2 hours.

2. Heat the ghee in a pan and gently brown the onions. Reducing the flame, add the garlic, ginger, chillies and tomatoes and cook for 2 minutes.

3. Add the meat along with its marinade. Pour the stock into the pan. Add the sugar and peppercorns, cover and cook for about 1½–2 hours on a low flame, until the meat is tender. Add more water if necessary.

4. Season with salt and lime juice. Garnish with parsley leaves.

Chicken in oyster sauce

1. Pour hot water over the dried jelly ear fungus and leave to stand for 20 minutes.

2. Blanch the broccoli in boiling, salted water for 2 minutes. Drain, rinse in cold water and drain thoroughly.

3. Cook the rice according to the pack instructions.

4. Heat the oil in a wok or frying pan. Add the chicken and brown quickly on a high flame. Add the onion, garlic, ginger, lemon grass and sambal oelek and fry for a further 3 minutes.

5. Slice the jelly ear fungus and add to the pan with the broccoli and ceps and stir-fry for 2 minutes.

6. Add the soy sauce, oyster sauce, stock and palm sugar and cook for 2 minutes.

7. Mix the cornflour with a little water and stir in to thicken the sauce. Add salt or soy sauce to taste.

Preparation time: 20 min
  plus 20 min standing
Cooking time: 10 min
Serves 4

25g dried jelly ear fungus
250g broccoli florets
250g basmati rice
4 tbsp oil
250g chicken breast fillet, cut into
  bite-sized pieces
1 small onion, finely chopped
2 garlic cloves, finely chopped
2cm piece ginger, finely chopped
½ tsp sambal oelek
3cm piece lemon grass, finely
  chopped
150g ceps, sliced
3 tbsp soy sauce
3 tbsp oyster sauce
50ml vegetable stock
1–2 tbsp palm sugar
1 tsp cornflour

Prawn pad thai

1. Cook the noodles according to the pack instructions. When cooked, drain and refresh in cold water. Devein the prawns by running a sharp knife down the back of the prawns and removing the dark brown intestinal vein with the tip of your knife.

2. Heat some oil in wok to a high temperature. Add the shallots and pickled turnip and stir-fry for 1. minute. Next add in the carrot and prawns and cook for about 1½ minutes or until the prawns have turned pink. Add the lime juice, tamarind, fish sauce and soy sauce and stir-fry for 30 seconds before add in the noodles.

3. Move the noodle mixture to one side of the wok and add the egg to the space left. Leave the egg for 30 seconds until just setting before combining and stirring through the noodles. Now add in the beansprouts and continue cooking for another minute, making sure the egg is cooked.

4. Sprinkle with the peanuts and garnish with fresh coriander.

Preparation time: 25 min
Cooking time: 10 min
Serves 4

170g flat pad Thai rice noodles
200g raw tiger prawns
oil, for frying
4 shallots, finely sliced
3 tbsp pickled turnip
2 carrots, cut into matchsticks
juice of 2 limes
2 tbsp tamarind paste
4 tbsp fish sauce
4 tbsp soy sauce
2 eggs, whisked
100g beansprouts
70g natural peanuts, unroasted or
    salted, roughly chopped

To garnish:
coriander

Teriyaki salmon ramen with rice noodles and spring onions

1. Pour the teriyaki sauce over the salmon, cover and set aside. Mix together the dressing ingredients. Steam the bok choy until just wilted.

2. Heat a non-stick frying pan and sear the salmon for 3 minutes on each side. Heat the chicken stock.

3. Take 4 large bowls and place some of the noodles, asparagus spears, shredded spring onions and a steamed bok choy in each. Pour over the hot stock and top each with a salmon fillet.

4. Finish by spooning some dressing over each salmon fillet.

Preparation time: 15 min
Cooking time: 6 min
Serves 4

8 tbsp teriyaki sauce
4 salmon fillets, skin removed
4 small bok choy
1 litre chicken stock
200g medium thickness rice noodles, cooked
12 asparagus spears, blanched
4 spring onions, shredded

Ramen dressing:
2 tbsp sweet chilli sauce
3 tbsp fish sauce
3cm piece of ginger, grated
juice of ½ lime

Vietnamese summer rolls

Preparation time: 10 min
Serves 10

10 medium dried rice paper
  wrapper
15 cooked tiger prawns, chopped
  in half diagonally
80g picked white crab meat
20g bean sprouts
¼ cucumber, cut into matchsticks
1 carrot, cut into matchsticks
2 spring onions, julienned
3 radishes, julienned
small bunch of basil
small bunch of mint

Dipping sauce:
30ml fish sauce
60ml water
30g sugar
30ml white wine vinegar
juice of ½ lime
1 garlic clove
1 red chilli, minced
1 grated shallot

1. Fill a deep-sided tray with warm water and add in a rice wrapper, leaving it for around 30 seconds until softened. Remove from the water and place on a board. Place 3 prawn halves on top of the wrapper, slightly off centre. Top with some crab, cucumber, bean sprouts, carrot, spring onions, radish and 2 basil leaves and 2 mint leaves.

2. Fold the sides of the wrapper in, followed by the bottom edge and roll as tightly as possible. Arrange on a plate with the prawns facing up.

3. To make the dipping sauce whisk together the dipping sauce ingredients and pour into a dipping bowl. Serve alongside the summer rolls.

Smoked salmon sushi with wasabi mayonnaise and pickled cucumber

1. Cook the sushi rice according to packet instructions. Allow to stand for 30 minutes uncovered. Mix the sliced cucumber and radish with the rice vinegar. Mix the wasabi with the mayonnaise.

2. Fill a small dipping bowl with half water and half sushi vinegar. Moisten the palm of your hand and finger with the water / vinegar mix. Take a small handful of the prepared sushi rice and mould into the shape of a block. Continue making blocks with the rice until you have around 12 blocks.

3. Chop the smoked salmon into strips the same size as your rice blocks and smear one side with some wasabi mayonnaise placed on top of the rice.

4. Serve with the pickled cucumber and radish and more wasabi mayonnaise.

Preparation time: 30 min
Cooking time: 10 min
Serves 12 pieces

170g sushi rice (weight before cooking)
70g cucumber, peeled and sliced
3 radishes, sliced
2 tbsp rice vinegar
2 tsp wasabi
2 tbsp mayonnaise
sushi vinegar
120g smoked salmon

Mixed vegetable bhaji with mint yoghurt

1. Chop the carrot and courgette into long thin strips and mix together with the red onion, green beans and ginger.

2. Mix the flours with the spices and whisk in the water, a little at a time, until you have produced a smooth batter.

3. Mix the yoghurt with the cumin, mint, salt and cucumber.

4. Pour the oil into a pan and heat until very hot. Mix a handful of the vegetables with the batter and drop this mixture into the hot oil. Continue mixing the vegetables with the batter and frying in small batches, removing the bahjis with a pair of tongs when they are golden and crispy. Drain off any excess oil by placing them on kitchen paper.

5. Place the bahjis on a large serving plate along with the mint yoghurt.

Preparation time: 10 min
Cooking time: 20 min
Serves 10

1 carrot
1 courgette
1 red onion, sliced
100g fine green beans
40g ginger, julienned
200ml sunflower oil

For the batter:
75g plain flour
75g garam flour
1 tsp turmeric
1 tsp fennel seeds
1 tsp garam masala
200ml water

For the mint yoghurt:
125g plain yoghurt
1 tsp ground cumin
2 tbsp chopped mint
pinch of salt
¼ cucumber, diced

Index